The
PROSPEROUS
Soul

STUDY GUIDE

The PROSPEROUS *Soul*

STUDY GUIDE

CINDY TRIMM

DESTINY IMAGE® PUBLISHERS, INC.

P.O. Box 310, Shippensburg, PA 17257-0310

"Promoting Inspired Lives."

This book and all other Destiny Image and Destiny Image Fiction books are available at Christian bookstores and distributors worldwide.

For more information on foreign distributors, call 717-532-3040.

Reach us on the Internet: www.destinyimage.com.

ISBN 13 TP: 978-0-7684-0521-7

For Worldwide Distribution, Printed in the U.S.A.

1 2 3 4 5 6 7 8 / 19 18 17 16 15

CONTENTS

WEEK 8
FINANCIAL PROSPERITY

INTRODUCTION FOR PARTICIPANTS

I am so excited about the 40-day journey ahead of us! If you have gone through any of the other studies so far—*The 40 Day Soul Fast* or *Reclaim Your Soul*—I am sure that you quickly discovered that all true transformation is a journey. This especially includes something so precious and so crucial as the transformation of your soul.

TRANSFORMATION IS A JOURNEY

Soul transformation is not instantaneous. A one-time prayer won't immediately launch you into living out of an authentic, prosperous soul. Although your spirit is immediately born again—or saved—once you pray (see Rom. 10:9), you are "transformed by the renewing of your mind" (Rom. 12:2) and must continue to "believe to the saving of the soul" (Heb. 10:39).

There are many things we are told to ask God for in the place of prayer—petitions we are invited to make before Him as the Sovereign Lord—but there are also divine strategies that He has provided in His Word that will yield extraordinary results in our lives. This is my vision for you as you go through this unique study. I want to give you strategies for a new season of living—a prosperous season. In fact, I want this next season to become the divine blueprint for the rest of your life!

THE JOURNEY SO FAR

If you have not yet participated in *The 40 Day Soul Fast* or *Reclaim Your Soul* studies, I highly recommend you make it a priority to go through those two series. At the same time, I want to encourage you to move forward with *The Prosperous Soul*. If you have a small group or church class that is embarking on this wonderful journey, by all means dive in with great joy and expectation. When you are finished here, you can go back and start with *The 40 Day Soul Fast*.

Briefly, *The 40 Day Soul Fast* shows you how to live more authentically, while *Reclaim Your Soul* empowers you to live more resiliently. Finally, you have *The Prosperous Soul*—the journey that you are getting ready to begin. This is your blueprint for living more abundantly.

Your Key to the Abundant Life

Over the next 40 days, I am going to give you a clear vision for what prosperity looks like in the eight realms of life—spiritual, emotional, intellectual, physical, relational, vocational, social, and financial. I will often make reference to *The Prosperous Soul* book and 40-day devotional, as these two resources provide you with practical ways you can make everyday choices that position you for a lifetime of abundance.

This study is different. The goal here is to give you the key to seeing transformation *sustained* in your life. Know this: I am not interested in just offering another book or another resource. I want to give you a vision that will help you sustain the very lifestyle these books and this study describe.

Here is the foundational Scripture verse that undergirds this journey:

> *Where there is no vision, the people perish* (Proverbs 29:18 KJV).

The Secret to Sustaining Soul Prosperity

Passion and vigor fade when there is no vision. In other words, when you do not have a clear vision for what prosperity looks like in your spiritual life, in your body, in your mind, in your relationships, in your workplace—if you are without clear vision, you will be without motivation.

It is so important for you to clearly see where you are going, for only that picture of total transformation can fuel your fire to keep going when it starts to get uncomfortable—when it becomes easy to neglect nourishing your body or fueling your mind—when it becomes convenient to settle for relationships that pull you down instead of take you to the next level—when it becomes comfortable to simply "coast" on yesterday's experiences with God, neglecting a habit of Scripture reading, meditation, and prayer. Again, it's easy for us to slip back into these default modes when we do not have a clear vision for where we are going.

YOUR BEST DAYS ARE AHEAD OF YOU!

Where you are going—the journey ahead—should be far more appealing than where you have been. Your best days are ahead of you! Know this. Believe it. Your best days are before you because as of today you will start implementing simple, daily practices that will completely reposition your life. Every step you take towards your destiny is a step you take *away* from where you have been. You are moving out of the old and into the new. Your today doesn't have to be a mirror image of your yesterday. I want this journey to create a holy discontentment within you to press on toward everything God has made available to you.

NEW DEFINITION, NEW DEMONSTRATION

For a while now, the Church has bought in to a very limited definition of prosperity. When there is a limited definition, there will be a limited demonstration. When we define prosperity as exclusively limited to finances, then that is the only form of prosperity we will either seek…or reject.

Jesus came to give you abundance in *every* area of life. I encourage you to let God's standard for prosperity redefine your paradigm. Embrace His definition. It is large. It is rich. It is satisfying. It is holistic. It impacts and energizes every area of your life. And the good news is that the same God who gives you vision for what soul prosperity looks like *empowers* you to walk in it!

Consider Jesus' vision for your life*: "I came so they can have real and eternal life, more and better life than they ever dreamed of"* (John 10:10 MSG).

Get ready for a 40-day journey that will show you what this *more and better* life looks like—and practice making it yours! After all, this is what Jesus always intended for you to enjoy. It's time to start taking Him at His Word and fully stepping into your inheritance.

Believing that your most prosperous days are ahead of you!

DR. CINDY TRIMM

HOW TO USE THIS STUDY GUIDE

WEEKLY GROUP SESSIONS

You can either join a group or pull together a group of your friends, sisters and brothers in the Lord, or colleagues. These individuals will make up your inner-circle support group that will provide invaluable insights and accountability as you work through the weekly activities. (See Eccles. 4:9-10; Ps. 133:1-3.)

Ideally, you will attend weekly sessions with your group or class. During this time, you will watch one of the eight DVD sessions, discuss what you learned, pray together, and participate in helpful empowerment exercises. In order to get the most out of your experience, you *must* be willing to go beyond information and open yourself up to transformation.

This happens through *participation*. Although participatory exercises are not always comfortable, the ones in this study have been crafted with your health and growth in mind. As we have learned throughout our experiences with *The 40 Day Soul Fast* and *Reclaim Your Soul* group studies, it is in the stretching—and sometimes squirming—that true growth and lasting freedom is achieved.

And, although the journey is intensely personal, it is in the sharing, the observing, the acknowledging, the trusting, and the humble and transparent relating with others who are all struggling, searching, believing, and hoping just like you. The vision of soul prosperity is most effectively and joyously cultivated in community.

SESSION STRUCTURE

Below is the set structure for each session in *The Prosperous Soul* study.

Summary

This is a short summary briefly introducing participants to that session's topic.

Learn

Watch Dr. Trimm's video teaching.

Discuss

Go through a series of *Group Discussion Questions*. These are structured intentionally, but are not all mandatory. If there is a certain question that seems to be directing the group/class sessions and the Holy Spirit is moving powerfully in that context, yield to His movement and stay on that particular subject.

Envision

After the *Group Discussion Questions*, allocate 10 to 15 minutes to do the envision exercise. This gives individuals and groups the opportunity to interact with what they have just learned. The key to success in this study is maintaining a clear vision of what prosperity looks like in each of the eight areas of life. In this section, it is important that each participant can clearly explain *what* prosperity truly looks like for each week's area of focus. Where there is no vision, people perish—and cast off restraint. Conversely, when there is vision for what spiritual prosperity, physical prosperity, and the others look like, participants will be more likely to practice the principles necessary for experiencing that vision of prosperity in their everyday lives.

Sustain

These are the *Daily Practice Exercises*. Depending on how much time you have, they can take from five to thirty minutes.

Daily Practice

The daily practice exercises are inspiring, brief thoughts meant to reinforce what you discovered in the video sessions. The material was written with one goal in mind—to help you *sustain* soul prosperity every day of your life.

The time required for each day's exercises will vary, although the reading and simple meditation shouldn't take more than five to ten minutes on any given day.

Start Prospering Now

Once again, to get the maximum impact from your *Prosperous Soul* experience, it is recommended that you spend ten to fifteen minutes focusing specifically on the *Start Prospering Now* activity at the end of each daily practice. Instead of giving you study questions, I want you to focus on *responding* and *activating*.

After the prompt, you will find ample writing space. This is designed to turn your "study guide" into a valuable personal resource. I envision this becoming a journal that, upon completion, does not end up resting on a shelf somewhere, but is a vital handbook for your ongoing transformation process.

The greatest jewels of revelation that fill this book will not be what is written in typed print, but the insights and reflections that you record during your journey.

THE PROSPEROUS SOUL: BOOK AND JOURNAL

This study is meant as a supplement to *The Prosperous Soul* book. To truly benefit from the study, you should read the book prior to doing the study (while working through the companion journal). This eight-week study is built on the principles presented in the book and journal. However, if this is not possible, the DVD study will still be meaningful and greatly beneficial if done in the context of a small group.

If this is the case for you, you might endeavor to read the book in conjunction with the study or shortly after completing the study. You will *not* get regurgitated, repackaged content. Yes, some of the concepts will be repeated. That is intentional for the purpose of reinforcement. However, each of *The Prosperous Soul* elements provide fresh revelation for experiencing prosperity, abundance, and true richness in all eight realms of life.

Beloved, I wish above all things that thou mayest prosper and be in health, even as thy soul prospereth.
—3 JOHN 2, KJV

Week 1

SPIRITUAL PROSPERITY

Change is not just a process, it is a Person.

Week One

GROUP EXERCISES

SUMMARY

Prosperity is not limited to finances; it impacts every area of our lives. In fact, you will discover that there are at least eight realms of life where you can walk in biblical prosperity. This eight-week journey is all about giving you a vision for what your life was *meant* to look like. However, the cornerstone to all true abundance is *Spiritual Prosperity*, the topic of emphasis in Week One. When you make the described spiritual disciplines (Scripture reading, prayer, meditation, fasting, and fellowship) everyday practices, you position your soul to enjoy the most lasting and satisfying prosperity there possibly is—a rich life with God.

LEARN

Watch Session 1: *Spiritual Prosperity.*

DISCUSS

1. How would you define prosperity?

2. Up until this point, what have been your impressions on prosperity—specifically, the idea that God wants you to prosper?

3. How is Dr. Trimm's approach to prosperity different than what you might have heard in the past?

4. Describe what prosperity is and what prosperity is not.

5. What are some Scriptures that describe the kind of prosperity that Dr. Trimm is talking about in this session?

6. How would you define spiritual prosperity?

7. Discuss the five practices of walking in spiritual prosperity.

8. Explain how each practice (Bible reading, prayer, meditation, fellowship, and fasting) can contribute to spiritual prosperity.

ENVISION

Briefly write down a vision for what prosperity in the following areas would look like for you. Be sure to write down *only one thing*, as there are five categories. Don't let this exercise overwhelm you. Don't feel pressured to make overnight changes in every one of these areas. You can start with one. And remember, this should be an enjoyable journey.

Describe your ideal vision for each of the following spiritual practices—how they would be integrated into your life and the incredible benefit they would be to your walk with God.

Bible Reading

_____

_____

_____

_____

_____

Prayer

_____

_____

_____
_____
_____

Meditation

_____
_____
_____
_____

Fasting

_____
_____
_____
_____

Fellowship

_____
_____
_____
_____

Day One

GOD'S WORD

*Receive and welcome the Word which
implanted and rooted [in your hearts]
contains the power to save your souls.*
—JAMES 1:21, AMP

PROSPERITY PRACTICE

Set aside daily time to read the Bible...and be creative!

God knows your schedule. You may have a completely free schedule where you can easily spend three to four hours reading the Bible every day. However, you may be a wife and mom with five children, and it is an absolute miracle if you are able to spend three minutes of quiet time in the Scriptures. I want to encourage you to pursue *quality* over quantity. Regardless of your schedule and level of busyness, this much I can promise: If the reward of reading God's Word is of value to you, you *will* figure out a way to do it.

At the same time, *be creative.* Although I agree it's important to set apart a place to sit and soak in the soul-transforming truths of God's Word, Scripture is Scripture. If you have to listen to an audio version of the Bible in your car, do it. If you have to lock yourself in the bathroom in the morning or evening for five minutes to read the Word, do it. If you have to spend time with God in the night before going to bed, do it. Don't become bound to a certain *way* of reading the Word. This is where something liberating and glorious can become legalistic. You are *not* reading the

Bible for God's sake or for His benefit; it is for you. Remember, it is the Word, which has the power to save and transform your soul! By making this investment, you position yourself to walk in wisdom, clarity, understanding, peace, joy, and every fruit of the Holy Spirit. God's Word is your personal constitution on how to live—and it also reminds you of everything that is available to you in Christ.

START PROSPERING NOW!

My plan for reading God's Word daily is:

_____

_____

_____

_____

_____

RECOMMENDED READING

Rick Warren's *Bible Study Methods*
Rick Renner's *Sparkling Gems from the Greek*

PROSPERITY MEDITATION

Our souls are the soil in which God
plants the seed of His Word.

PROSPERITY DECLARATION

Lord, I give myself to Your Word every day! Thank You for making Your great and precious promises known to me in its pages. Your Word reveals my rich inheritance in Jesus Christ. Holy Spirit, help me to understand what God has made freely available to me and empower me to walk in Your prosperity every day of my life!

Day Two

PRAYER

Pray without ceasing.
—1 Thessalonians 5:17, esv

Prosperity Practice

Make prayer a lifestyle.

It is amazing to hear how many Christians struggle with this concept of a "quiet time" or practicing a daily devotional habit. Unfortunately, the practice of prayer has become something that, for whatever reason, we feel obligated to fulfill rather than a lifestyle to be enjoyed. Today, I want to help you shift your perspective on prayer. A new vision of prayer is the only thing that will keep you *praying*. If it remains a duty, it will continue to be a drudgery. Oh, but when you start seeing prayer as the delight it is, everything will change!

Do you want to walk in spiritual prosperity? One thing that will prevent you from doing this is defining prayer as some kind of obligatory practice that keeps God happy with you. That can be more oppressive than liberating! Nor is prayer a mindless "Hi there, God" in the morning, or "Now I lay me down to sleep..." at night. Prayer, as defined by the Bible, is a lifestyle of talking to and hearing from God. Period. This is why Paul was able to walk in such intimacy with the Lord. His spiritual prosperity was not accidental; it was the result of a man who set his will to *pray without ceasing*. His letters to the Ephesians and Philippians leave one awestruck at the level of closeness Paul enjoyed with God.

I have good news for you: Deep intimacy with God is not just for the spiritual elite. It is not just for the Pauls, Peters, and apostles of old. You can enjoy life-changing closeness with God *today*. Just remember, He is only a conversation away.

START PROSPERING NOW!

After watching Dr. Trimm's session and reading your daily devotional, what does a lifestyle of *prayer without ceasing* look like to you?

_____

_____

_____

_____

_____

PROSPERITY MEDITATION

God likes hanging out with us more
than we could ever imagine.

PROSPERITY DECLARATION

Prayer is not an obligation. It is not boring. It is not my spiritual duty. It is my delight and privilege. Father, You want to talk to me all of the time and You enjoy spending time with me. You are always speaking. Thank You for helping me tune my spiritual ears to always be listening for—and hearing— Your voice.

MEDITATION

*This Book of the Law shall not depart from your
mouth, but you shall meditate in it day and night,
that you may observe to do according to all that
is written in it. For then you will make your way
prosperous, and then you will have good success.*
—JOSHUA 1:8

PROSPERITY PRACTICE

Find Scriptures to meditate on!

Biblical meditation is not about emptying the mind, as is the case with Eastern practices. Far from it. It is actually a call to *fill* and *saturate* your mind with the soul-renewing Word of God. We cannot read the Bible just for information. There are many in the world weighed down with biblical information. They may be masters of theology, but they are living defeated lives. Why? They are not practicing meditation.

Remember, quantity and quality are different. It is not about reading entire chapters and books of the Bible in order to feel spiritually accomplished. It is not about how much you read, but how much you are able to seed into your spirit and practice. Meditation helps you deeply absorb the wisdom of God. When you are able to retain what you read in the Bible, you are then able to use the truth you meditated on like a sword against circumstances that come against you. When you deal with situations in life that Scripture has answers for, you can draw from that deep well of the Word *within your mind.* Meditation is responsible for what Paul describes in Romans 12:2 as "*the renewing of your mind.*" Your mind is actually transformed through the process of meditation. No longer do you think like everyone else in the world, but you start to think like God. After all, the very thing you are meditating on, the Bible, is a blueprint of God's thoughts! Information alone does not do this. We need to take that information and mull it over and over and over again in our minds. We need to reflect on it. Write it out. Contemplate. Consider. Wrestle. Such is not typically encouraged in our society today.

Memorization and meditation are different. When you memorize a passage of Scripture, you are able to quote it on demand. When you meditate upon a passage of Scripture, you might not be able to quote it exactly, but you are able to firmly stand on its truth, its promise, and its principle.

START PROSPERING NOW!

Are your thoughts in alignment with God's Word?

I want to give you two highly practical tools to evaluate whether or not your thoughts are worth meditating on. Use the following two standards to measure what thoughts are acceptable for you to think upon.

1. **The Fruit of the Spirit.** Are your thoughts full of the following?

   Love, joy, peace, longsuffering, kindness, goodness, faithfulness, gentleness, self-control (Galatians 5:22-23).

2. **The Quality of Meditation.** Are your thoughts characterized by the following?

   Whatever things are true, whatever things are noble, whatever things are just, whatever things are pure, whatever things are lovely, whatever things are of good report, if there is any virtue and if there is anything praiseworthy—meditate on these things (Philippians 4:8).

Find a Scripture and start meditating on it! You can start with Joshua 1:8, or any other passage that specifically relates to biblical meditation. Think about it. Write down your thoughts in the following lined space. Consider what your life would look like *if* you started thinking like this Scripture instructs you to.

PROSPERITY MEDITATION

Some of the greatest thinkers, from Isaac Newton to R.G. Letourneau, were men of both faith and science who constantly asked God to increase their understanding in order to improve their world. By mixing their thoughts about God with the questions that puzzled them, their meditations transformed lives.

PROSPERITY DECLARATION

I meditate on that which is true, noble, just, pure, lovely, of good report, virtuous, and praiseworthy. Any thought that comes into my mind that brings fear, anxiety, worry, lust, envy, pride, or any attitude or feeling that is contrary to Your Word, I cast it down. It is an imagination that opposes the knowledge of Christ and is not welcome in my mind. I meditate on Your Word. As I focus on Your thoughts, Lord, they will transform the way I think and meditate, and will empower me to live the prosperous life You have made available!

Day Four

FASTING

*Moreover, when you fast, do not be like the hypocrites,
with a sad countenance. For they disfigure their faces
that they may appear to men to be fasting. Assuredly,
I say to you, they have their reward. But you, when
you fast, anoint your head and wash your face, so
that you do not appear to men to be fasting, but
to your Father who is in the secret place; and your
Father who sees in secret will reward you openly.*
—MATTHEW 6:16-18

PROSPERITY PRACTICE

Make fasting a regular spiritual practice.

Fasting is often directly connected to *breakthrough*. Why is this the case? Fasting de-clutters your life so you are able to clearly hear and discern the voice of God. As you temporarily abstain from certain things (be it food, entertainment, social media), you are expressing a desire to tune in to Heaven's frequency at a greater level. Every so often, we need to do this. It helps us to spiritually recalibrate. No, you don't need to fast in order to hear the voice of God. At the same time, if you have *not* been hearing God's voice clearly, I would strongly recommend a time of fasting, as it is during these times where the Holy Spirit lovingly reveals what barriers have been hindering us from deeper communion with God.

People often experience significant breakthroughs on the other side of their fasts simply because they removed the hindrances or distractions that were keeping them from hearing God's voice. When you intentionally remove what might be coming between you and being fully present with the Lord, everything becomes clearer. When you can hear God's voice, you are able to discern what He is saying concerning your circumstances, your life situations, your prayer requests, your needs, etc. You begin to get God's perspective. You begin to hear Heaven's solutions. This empowers you to pray with a greater level of power and authority, for when you know what God is saying—and start declaring what He is *already* speaking—you are aligning your prayers with the very heartbeat of Father God. This consistently produces miraculous results, often greater than you can hope, dream, or imagine.

You may go into a time of fasting with some level of expectation of what you desire God to do in your life. You will be amazed to see how He takes your hopes, dreams, and requests and significantly upgrades them. Often, it is in the place of fasting where we discover that we were asking too small!

Start Prospering Now!

Choose a day this week for your fast, stick to it, and write down your progress in the following pages. This will serve as your initial *fasting journal*. I encourage you to keep a journal every time you fast, writing down what God says to you and capture your experiences with Him. Keep track of how God speaks to you and also the condition of your heart toward matters of the spirit. Fasting does *nothing* for God; remember, it is all about positioning *your soul* to experience Him in a new, fresh way!

Come up with your plan for a fast below. Write down the date that would work best for you. Also, do your best to organize your schedule *around* the fast. Many people fail with fasts because of lack of preparation and foresight.

_____

_____

_____

_____

RESOURCES ON FASTING

I have provided some exceptional resources below that give further instruction regarding *how* to fast and powerful insights about the benefits that fasting will bring to your walk with God.

- Jentezen Franklin, *Fasting*
- Elmer Towns, *Fasting for Spiritual Breakthrough: A Guide to Nine Biblical Fasts*
- Mahesh Chavda, *The Hidden Power of Prayer and Fasting*
- Derek Prince, *Shaping History Through Prayer and Fasting*

PROSPERITY MEDITATION

When we fast, we put ourselves into the hands
of the Father so He might prune away the
things that are hindering our success—all so
we can be more fruitful and prosper.

PROSPERITY DECLARATION

As I get ready to fast this week, I am believing You, God, for a breakthrough. Strengthen me, Holy Spirit, not to approach this fast like I might have in the past. It is not a ritual; it is an opportunity for me to encounter You in a new and fresh way. You are the breakthrough that I hunger and thirst for, Lord. Teach me the value of fasting and show me how it positions me to live in greater levels of spiritual abundance and soul prosperity.

FASTING JOURNAL

Day Five

FELLOWSHIP

*As iron sharpens iron, so a man sharpens
the countenance of his friend.*
—Proverbs 27:17

PROSPERITY PRACTICE

Assemble with people who, spiritually, you wish to resemble.

The topic of relationships is so prevalent and important that we are going to take an entire week to review it in greater detail. For now, I want you to understand how important your circle of fellowship is to your spiritual prosperity. In fact, the people with whom you are in continuous, close fellowship often serve as indicators of where you are—and where you are headed—spiritually speaking.

Take a moment to analyze your closest circle of friends. Seriously pause and reflect on their lives. Do you want to go in the same direction that they are headed in? More specifically, are their spiritual lives enviable to you? Do they sharpen you and cause you to pursue God with even greater passion and vigor? Or do they trivialize their relationship with God? Maybe they are "Christians" in name only. Perhaps they even go to church, but the Jesus they confess on Sunday morning and the lives they live Monday through Saturday are not one and the same.

We need to strongly protect our inner circle of fellowship. The people we spend the most consistent time with and form the deepest relationships with are actually projections of where we are going in life. Make sure they are people who can take you to the next level in your relationship with God!

START PROSPERING NOW!

This week, ask God to change the way you view fellowship *and* to help you build your existing communities. Pray:

God, what are some practical ways that I can enrich the fellowship I am currently experiencing? How can I take it to the next level in my friendships, relationships, and church community?

Evaluate your current inner circle of fellowship. Are these relationships causing you to draw closer to God or drift away? Consider their spiritual lives and write down the characteristics that encourage you to mature in your relationship with Christ.

PROSPERITY MEDITATION

Within God's mysteries are the answers that
our world needs. If we are to meet those needs,
we have to plumb the depths of God together
and dig those solutions out—together.

PROSPERITY DECLARATION

Fellowship is more than going to church; it is about me being the Church. Father, I believe You want to strengthen my relationships and my church community. Show me what I can bring to the table that will add power to my relationships and bring our fellowship to new levels.

Week 2

INTELLECTUAL PROSPERITY

You are only as strong as the truth that you know

Week Two

GROUP EXERCISES

SUMMARY

While most of us have been taught the importance of building spiritual prosperity—particularly the importance of reading the Bible—it is also vital that we develop intellectually. Scripture reveals, time after time, that the mind is very important. It is what casts down arguments that are opposed to the knowledge of God (see 2 Cor. 10:4-5). The mind determines who we are and what we become (see Prov. 23:7). A renewed mind is a prosperous mind, and a prosperous mind thinks in alignment with God's thoughts (see Rom. 12:2). There are many ways that you can cultivate intellectual prosperity in your life. In this session, you will receive a vision for what abundance looks like in the area of your mind, as well as learning the keys to experiencing its blessing in your life!

LEARN

Watch Session 2: *Intellectual Prosperity.*

DISCUSS

1. What result could intellectual prosperity produce in your life?

2. Why do you think the mind is so important to how you live?

3. Review the following Scripture verses and explain how each one reminds us why intellectual prosperity is so important:

- 2 Corinthians 10:4-5
- Proverbs 23:7, KJV
- Romans 12:2

4. Describe how God's laws are a blessing to our lives and not a hindrance.

5. Discuss: What "keys to experiencing intellectual prosperity" stood out to you the most during Dr. Trimm's session? Why?

6. How is growing the mind/intellect comparable to building muscle?

7. What does it mean to operate in your intellectual capacity?

ENVISION

Describe what intellectual prosperity looks like to you.

Briefly write down a vision for what prosperity in the following areas would look like for you. Be sure to write down *only one thing*, as there are five categories. Don't let this exercise overwhelm you. Don't feel pressured to make overnight changes in every one of these areas. You can start with one. Take it slow and enjoy the journey. Describe your ideal vision for each of the following practices—how they might be integrated into your life and how they would prosper you intellectually.

Reading

Focus

Creativity

Study

Wisdom

Day Six

READING

The more that you read, the more things you will know.
The more that you learn, the more places you'll go.
—Dr. Seuss

PROSPERITY PRACTICE

Make reading books an everyday event!

Reading puts you at an incredible advantage. It increases your intellectual capacity for knowledge. This is why I encourage you to read books not only about subjects that interest you, but also about topics you know nothing about. In fact, intentionally read books about what you do not know so that you can begin your journey to knowing.

Books prosper you intellectually because they are adders. They add information. They add inspiration. They add encouragement. They add strategy. They add creativity. They add expertise. They add skills. They add to innate talents and develop them further. They add clarity, sharpness, and wisdom. The list is endless. The bottom line is that books are important resources that help build your intellectual capacity.

START PROSPERING NOW!

Select books that are on topics that are of interest to you—and on subjects that you would like to learn more about. Challenge yourself. Take a trip to your local bookstore, go to the library, seek the advice of friends or experts, browse online—explore those topics and titles that have always intrigued you!

List your book titles here so you have an idea of where you will be going. Plan to read at least one book a month, and then schedule your reading for the next several months. Even if you don't have a title, write down a subject or topic you would be interested in reading about:

Start somewhere. Devote yourself to reading one chapter, ten pages, or for only fifteeen minutes each day—you will reap exponential returns on your investment!

PROSPERITY MEDITATION

There is wealth in books of all kinds, because the
love of learning is a key element of prosperity.

PROSPERITY DECLARATION

I grow in intellectual wealth as I begin the habit of reading every day. Lord, give me direction for what I should be reading and help me stick to my reading plan. Holy Spirit, ever remind me how reading builds my mind, enriches my creativity, and helps me develop into the rich soul You desire me to be.

Day Seven

FOCUS

Lack of direction, not lack of time, is the
problem. We all have twenty-four hour days.
—ZIG ZIGLAR

PROSPERITY PRACTICE

Be careful to say "No" to good things so that you can say "Yes" to great things.

Successful people are focused people. I can't help but think of Steve Jobs. This man, who completely revolutionized technology and the computer industry, has been quoted saying, "Focusing is about saying 'No.'" I am sure he was constantly presented with multiple opportunities—many of which probably sounded very appealing! But at the day's end, Jobs' key to focus was his discipline to say "No" to lesser or even good things so that he could say "Yes" to the best things. Turns out that those "best" things would change the world!

The apostle Paul also comes to mind. I talk about him in the session as a stunning example of focus, as it was he who wrote, *"But one thing I do,"* describing the forward direction in his journey with God. *One thing.* Not two. Not three. Not ten. He was focused.

Two sisters, Mary and Martha, had the privilege of hosting Jesus in their home. While Mary sat at Jesus' feet listening to Him speak, Martha was busy in the kitchen serving. Jesus does not applaud this. He counted it as a distraction, explaining to Martha: *"Martha, Martha, you are worried and troubled about many things"* (Luke 10:41).

What was the source of Martha's worries and troubles? Focusing on *many things* when only *one thing* was truly needed. Mary was a woman of one thing—a powerful example of focus.

START PROSPERING NOW!

Take a few moments to write a list of everything you are presently doing/focused on *right now.* This can range from family to business to hobbies. This would include everything that is currently taking up time and mental energy in your life.

My Focus List:

Once you have written everything down, I want you to prayerfully review your list. Ask yourself, "What demands my 'Yes' and what is a distraction?" This will help you evaluate what priorities you need to be focused on right now, and what you may need to put to the side or schedule for a future season. Write a "Yes" next to the key things you need to stay focused on. Everything else should be removed from the list and placed into a different category. This is not a call to delete the other things; it is simply a tool to help you evaluate what you must focus on *right now,* and what can be done at a later time.

PROSPERITY MEDITATION

Most successful people don't do a dozen little
things well, but find one true calling, cut away the
distractions, and pour their hearts into doing that
one thing better than anyone else in the world.

PROSPERITY DECLARATION

I give my "Yes" to the most important things. I say "No" to every distraction that tries to steal my attention from what You want me to be focused on in this season. I have eyes that are trained to see what You are doing and how You are moving. Whatever I am called to focus on, I give myself fully and wholly to accomplish it with excellence. No more distractions!

Day Eight

CREATIVITY

*Every child is an artist. The problem is
staying an artist when you grow up.*
—PABLO PICASSO

PROSPERITY PRACTICE

Work out your creative muscles every day!

It is not bad to color inside the lines. I know teachers regularly encourage their students to do this, along with many other activities that are purposed to reinforce the need for structure. Without structure, there is anarchy. However, I believe we desperately need to balance our insistence upon structure with a liberty to be creative—and yes, on occasion, color *outside of the lines.*

When considering those who dared to be creative, I have to go back to Steve Jobs. He is a prime example of one who dreamed and, as a result, dared to go beyond what was accepted as *the way it's always been.* Has it ever occurred to you that the way it's always been might need to change? We should never stop searching for how to do new things—or for new ways of doing old things. This is the genesis of innovation—and entire movements, such as the Renaissance, the Industrial Revolution, and the Information Age.

Practice creativity every day. Unfortunately, the creative muscles for many of us have atrophied over the years. The good news is they can be strengthened by exercise. Get a vision for how important creativity is in your life. Who knows? Maybe on the other side of your creativity is an idea or invention that could change the world!

START PROSPERING NOW!

Decide that you are going to exercise your creative muscles in some way *every day*! You'll never know what you are capable of until you step out and put your creativity to work. This may be your time to revisit old hobbies or talents that have been dormant for years—or even decades. Perhaps it's playing music, writing poetry, acting, painting, building, designing, gardening, knitting, drawing, tinkering under the hood of your car—whatever it is, start putting it to work and discover how amazingly creative God has made you to be!

Write down some areas where you would like to develop your creativity.

_____

_____

_____

_____

_____

_____

_____

In what simple ways can you practice creativity in your life *every day*?

_____

_____

_____

PROSPERITY MEDITATION

God created you for a specific reason, and His world is not complete without what He designed you to contribute to it. Never underestimate the power and importance of your own creativity.

PROSPERITY DECLARATION

I was created in the image of Creator God! This means I am creative. I have a creative muscle, and every day I will exercise it. Holy Spirit, You are the Author of creativity. Show me what I am capable of as I step out and start creating. Help me to press past any feelings of discouragement or inferiority and start putting my creativity to work.

Day Nine

STUDY

It is a mistake to think that the practice of my art has become easy to me. I assure you, dear friend, no one has given so much care to the study of composition as I. There is scarcely a famous master in music whose works I have not frequently and diligently studied.
—WOLFGANG AMADEUS MOZART

PROSPERITY PRACTICE

Studying positions you for new levels of intellectual prosperity.

When you commit to study a certain subject, you are setting out on a quest that ultimately leads to intellectual prosperity. Studying is not being idle with information; it is a relentless pursuit of knowledge that is designed to build your intellectual capacity.

Most of us were taught to study for tests and exams in school. This perspective permeates our approach to study starting in grade school and does not end until we reach the highest level of education possible. It is one thing to study to get an "A" on a test; it is another thing to integrate good study habits into our everyday life routines. The problem with academic study is that, in many cases, once our objective is reached, the information begins to dissipate. We find ourselves unable to retain the information that we spent hours, perhaps even weeks, committing to memory. Why? Because after taking our tests, we conclude that we've fulfilled our obligation to learning and thus have no more practical use for the information acquired.

But what if we studied for life? The good news is that it does not have to be an all-night cram session. Rather, studying can become a way of living. It is all about identifying those topics that you want to learn more about, pursuing knowledge with tenacity, and committing the newfound information to your memory.

As you will discover tomorrow, studying creates an intellectual well for wisdom to draw from!

START PROSPERING NOW!

When you identify key topics that you wish to study, this adds a whole new level of intentionality to your life. You no longer wander aimlessly from one thing to the next, being a novice at many things, but a master at none. Remember, it's not about studying to know a lot about everything, but only what is of most interest to you—or what will help you solve a dilemma or improve your effectiveness. It's about unraveling a ball of yarn—or peeling the onion, if you will—that God has put into your soul. Like the childhood story of Hansel and Gretel, it is following the trail of breadcrumbs He has laid out that leads to your real passion and purpose. It is what you are wired for, and where your greatest happiness and satisfaction lies.

So ask yourself:

- "What topics/disciplines would I like to become more of an expert in?"

- "What interests me?"

- "What am I passionate about?"

- "What do I want to learn?"

Use the next page to brainstorm some of these ideas by writing them out.

STUDYING NOTES

PROSPERITY MEDITATION

There are things you need to know to fulfill your calling on the earth, and the key to unlocking them is to learn to dig deeply into what interests you—what will make you an expert, or what will help answer the questions that seize your heart.

PROSPERITY DECLARATION

Studying takes me from one level to the next. It is my doorway into abundance and intellectual prosperity! Any negative ideas or thoughts that I have had about studying in the past, I lay those down. Instead, I see studying as a tool that leads me right into my destiny and created purpose. It unlocks the areas that I am most interested in and those topics that I have been called to specialize in.

Day Ten

WISDOM

The one who gets wisdom loves life; the one who
cherishes understanding will soon prosper.
—PROVERBS 19:8, NIV

PROSPERITY PRACTICE

Wisdom draws from the well of knowledge you build through study.

Wisdom is your divine key to enjoying prosperity in all eight areas of life! It is one thing to *know* about something—it is another thing entirely to practice what you know and watch it produce results. Results require wisdom. There are many people who possess a great deal of information and knowledge, but they lack the wisdom to practically apply it. Application is what creates results.

This is exactly what wisdom does. It takes the knowledge that we build through study and turns it into a currency that produces results. Think about it. Studying to accumulate information provides a base. Wisdom relies on that well of information to draw from. If we do not have information, wisdom does not have substance to work with. Studying creates the well; wisdom draws from it. We need both, yes. But studying is not the ultimate; wisdom is. Heed the invitation of Proverbs 4:7: "*Getting wisdom is the wisest thing you can do!*" (NLT). Einstein said that wisdom "is not a product of schooling but of the lifelong attempt to acquire it."

Once more, acquiring information through study is important because of the knowledge base it produces in our lives. However, without wisdom, that information sits in our minds like a stagnant pond. It either evaporates, or worse, starts to stink when we go around making a spectacle of how much we know. Truly wise people don't need to do this, for how much they know is revealed in how they live.

START PROSPERING NOW!

Write down areas where you need wisdom in your life *right now*. These could be different situations, circumstances, relationships, ideas, strategies, etc. Keep in mind, wisdom is not just something that helps us navigate through difficulty; it also gives us the upper hand and supernatural advantage of coming up with new ideas and innovative strategies.

I am providing two categories for you to consider. Write down the different situations where you need wisdom, and then simply ask God, in accordance with James 1:5, to generously give it to you.

Circumstances/Situations That Need Supernatural Solutions

These would fall more into the "problem" category, where you need wisdom to help you come up with an answer, give you strength to get through, provide counsel to someone going through difficulty, etc. *Write down the item that you need wisdom for and then, beneath it, write down what the Holy Spirit speaks to you concerning it.*

Ideas/Strategies That Need Supernatural Execution

This category is proactive, not reactive. You are asking the Holy Spirit to give you wisdom for ideas, inventions, creative strategies, business plans, etc., that you might never have even considered. *Write down the idea and then, in the space below, write down any direction or wisdom that the Holy Spirit gives you concerning that specific idea.*

PROSPERITY MEDITATION

The wisdom of God comes as we steadfastly follow Him, listen for His voice, and obey what we hear. When we let His principles inform our decision-making and allow Him to show us the way He sees things, wisdom comes in ways we would never expect.

PROSPERITY DECLARATION

Father, You give wisdom freely and generously! I am not lacking for wisdom; I believe You give it to me as I simply ask in faith. So Lord, I come once again and ask You to fill me with Your supernatural wisdom. Enable me to take information and apply it, both to navigate through difficult situations and also to unlock the creativity and innovation that You placed within me.

Week 3

EMOTIONAL PROSPERITY

Control your emotions in order to
gain control over your life.

Week Three

GROUP EXERCISES

SUMMARY

Emotional prosperity is truly something that all of us desire to walk in…*and enjoy*! This is the ability to control our emotions instead of allowing our emotions to have control *over* us. The first thing we need to understand is that emotions are not evil; they were wired into us by the Creator Himself. In fact, Scripture reveals time after time where God displays His emotions. He feels. He weeps. He laughs. To be the emotional creatures that we were designed to be and live with our emotions *in balance*, it is important for us to follow God's example. In order to be emotionally prosperous people, we need to follow some essential steps that position us for abundance in this area.

LEARN

Watch Session 3: *Emotional Prosperity.*

DISCUSS

1. What areas of your life would emotional prosperity include?

2. Why is it important to know the difference between a Jezebel and a "control freak"?

3. Review the story of Mary and Martha in Luke 10:38-42:

- In what ways could Mary be described as being emotionally prosperous?

- In what ways could Martha be described as lacking emotional prosperity?

- What does Jesus communicate to both women about walking in emotional prosperity?

4. How can being a controlling person prevent you from enjoying emotional prosperity?

   - What are some common areas of control that we often don't even recognize in our lives?

5. In what ways does competition harm us emotionally?

6. Discuss how being critical (to ourselves and others) is emotionally harmful.

7. Which of the "keys to experiencing emotional prosperity" was most relevant to your life?

8. How can you begin controlling your emotions?

ENVISION

Describe what emotional prosperity looks like to you.

Briefly write down a vision for what prosperity in the following areas would look like for you. Be sure to write down *only one thing*, as there are five categories. Don't let this exercise overwhelm you. Don't feel pressured to make overnight changes in every one of these areas. You can start with one. Again this should be a rejuvenating, not burdensome, journey. Describe your ideal vision for each of the following practices—how these might be integrated into your life and how they would prosper you emotionally.

Joy

_____

_____

_____

_____

_____

Peace

_____

_____

_____

_____

_____

Fortitude

_____

_____

_____

_____

_____

Hope

_____

_____

_____

_____

_____

Tenacity

_____

_____

_____

_____

_____

Day Eleven

JOY

You will show me the path of life; In
Your presence is fullness of joy.
—PSALM 16:11

PROSPERITY PRACTICE

Be intentional to spend time in God's presence, for it is here that you experience true, lasting joy.

Everything about the prosperous soul is a journey. For example, there is a journey to *enjoying* joy. If you have the Spirit of God living inside of your spirit, you have the seed of joy living inside of you. This means you don't need to cry out, begging God, "Please, give me joy." Joy is readily available in Christ—Jesus said, *"These things I have spoken to you, that My joy may remain in you, and that your joy may be full"* (John 15:11). It's already seeded in your spirit. The journey of the prosperous soul is the ultimate *inside-out* adventure. To tap into that "joy of the Lord," so to speak, you must pursue intimacy with the Holy Spirit; that fellowship will stir your well of joy and cause it to surface.

When you spend time in God's presence, you spend time with the One who has placed joy within you. He will show you what it looks like, how to live under its influence, and how to enjoy it every single day of your life. We experience *true* joy in the presence of God, as David explains in Psalm 16:11. If we can experience joy in God's presence, than it stands to reason that we also receive strength in God's presence. Scripture tells us that the joy of the

Lord is our strength (see Neh. 8:10). Only God Himself gives your soul a joy that is *"unspeakable and full of glory"* (1 Pet. 1:8 KJV).

START PROSPERING NOW!

Remember, you *possess* joy! It's time that you started making withdrawals from the joy account that Christ has deposited in your spirit. I repeat, joy is something you already possess. Now, I want you to begin experiencing this joy in your emotions. Although joy itself is not an emotion, as it is not a fleeting feeling—nor is it conditional—the joy of the Lord will *definitely* impact your emotions.

Joy comes from God and is unshakable. Acknowledge it. Pursue it. And then, receive the supernatural strength that comes from the very joy of God within you!

1. I acknowledge that joy is a fruit of the Spirit—it is not a feeling or emotional response. (See Galatians 5:22-23.)

2. I pursue God's presence expecting to be filled with the fullness of joy, and I choose to live aware of His presence every single day. (See Psalm 16:11.)

3. I receive strength from God's joy as I allow His joy to empower me to walk through every trial, circumstance, and situation. (See Nehemiah 8:10.) I will not be overcome or overwhelmed; my eyes are on God's goodness and I choose to be more aware of Him than my circumstances.

When you enter God's presence, remember that in His presence is fullness of joy. It's not so much about looking for a place where God's presence is; rather, it is about pausing and remembering that God's very Spirit dwells *within you.* You are His house, His tabernacle, His dwelling place. If His presence is within you—and His presence contains fullness of joy—meditate on the fact that the source of all joy is within you. Write down what you experience today as you enter in and discover God's joy.

Write down your reflections:

_____

_____

_____

_____

_____

PROSPERITY MEDITATION

Happiness happens to us; joy comes from living
for something greater than ourselves.

PROSPERITY DECLARATION

Father, in Your presence is fullness of joy! I choose to be more aware of who You are—Great, Mighty, Faithful, and All-Powerful—than I am of my present situations or struggles. I lift my eyes above what I see in the natural, for what I am going through is temporary; who You are is eternal and unchanging. You are my joy, Lord. Your joy is my strength, and I trust that Your joy will empower me to overcome and experience victory.

Day Twelve

PEACE

And the peace of God, which surpasses all understanding,
will guard your hearts and minds through Christ Jesus.
—PHILIPPIANS 4:7

PROSPERITY PRACTICE

Peace protects your heart and mind, bringing stability to your soul.

This Scripture makes a very powerful point concerning the soul's need for peace. Peace is absolutely necessary in your life if you want to enjoy emotional prosperity, because it *guards* your heart and mind from the feelings, thoughts, and influences that would attempt to throw your soul off balance. How is this possible? Revisit Paul's words above and then consider his context. If any person in history had reason to live in a state of emotional turmoil, it was Paul the apostle. One cannot venture too far into reading his epistles without being graphically confronted with the numerous hardships that he faced—shipwreck, torture, persecution, abandonment, accusation, being left for dead, etc. Yet, through it all, the same Paul wrote of a divine peace that protects our hearts and minds *through Christ Jesus.* Here is what peace does. Peace sets before our hearts and minds every single promise and every truth that Jesus declared. The words of Jesus are vital to our emotional prosperity, as they keep our feelings anchored in the midst of turbulent circumstances. When our emotions are given reason to become unsettled and unstable, the peace of God brings to our minds and hearts remembrance of who

Jesus is (the very Prince of Peace), what He has said, and what He will do. These truths become anchors for our emotions.

START PROSPERING NOW!

The greatest source of peace comes in remembering what Jesus did for you on the Cross. As you remember this history-defining sacrifice, you will begin to experience a peace that *passes all understanding* and that guards your mind and heart in Christ.

Let me present you a few simple questions for your consideration. Answer honestly, as this will evaluate whether or not you are experiencing the peace He has made abundantly available to your soul:

1.   How do you see God? Is He faithful or unreliable? He must be faithful in order for you to believe His promises and walk in His supernatural peace.

2.   How do you see yourself? Are you the product of some cosmic clockmaker who simply wound you up and forgot about you, or are you the unique creation of a loving Father who has a distinct purpose for your life? If you don't believe you are significant to God, then you will see His promises as off limits and have difficulty walking in peace.

3. How do you see your salvation? Are you truly, fully, and completely saved, or do you think that every time you make a mistake or mess up you run the risk of becoming disowned by the Savior? How you answer this question is telling of how you view your position before God. You need to know that Jesus' blood has made you righteous, placing you in right standing before God Almighty. If you don't wholeheartedly believe this, you will constantly be working to become righteous and never enjoy the peace that comes because Jesus performed the work of righteousness on your behalf.

PROSPERITY MEDITATION

Embrace peace as a firm foundation
upon which to prosper your soul.

PROSPERITY DECLARATION

Father, You are good, You are faithful, and You are reliable. You never change, and I can trust in Your promises. They are available to me because I am Your child. Because of Jesus, I stand righteous in Your sight. I may not be perfect. I may mess up and make mistakes. Still, You love me. Thank You for Your grace. Thank You that Jesus' blood has made me right before you, and because of this I can walk in supernatural peace every single day of my life.

Day Thirteen

FORTITUDE

*The grass withers, the flower fades, but
the word of our God stands forever.*
—Isaiah 40:8

PROSPERITY PRACTICE

Make the eternal Word of God your final authority for evaluating your feelings and emotions.

I want us to start exploring some *positive* emotions. When it comes to the subject of emotional prosperity, immediately we bring to mind all of the emotions and feelings that are out of control in our lives. While we definitely need to address these, we must also establish new emotional patterns *replacing* the imbalance if we are going to enjoy the wholeness that God desires us to walk in. Fortitude is a key to sustaining wholeness. It is a strength that comes through stability and this stability comes from *the Word of our God.*

Over the last few days, we have been looking at a few ways that God desires to stabilize our often fickle emotions. Joy and peace serve as emotional anchors, but in order for both to have full impact, we must embrace a "settled, established, immovable" perspective when it comes to the Word of God. Fortitude is developed by building your emotions upon what is eternal—the Word and promises of God. The Bible cannot be a book of suggestions or maybes; it must be truth we are willing to stake our lives upon. In fact, we discover that Scripture is exalted even above the Name of God. In Psalm 138:2, we see that God "*hast magnified thy word above all thy name*" (KJV). What does this mean? For us to even have a context for who God is (His Name), it is important that we are firmly grounded in His Word. Scripture shows us God's nature and character. He will never act in opposition to who He is. How do we know who He is and what He is like? This has been revealed to us through the Bible. The words of God reinforce the Name of God. What He says and what He does reveals who He is. And when you build your life upon the very Word that reveals the identity and nature of God, you are building on steady ground!

START PROSPERING NOW!

Write down situations that you are currently dealing with that are causing you to feel strong emotions. This may seem like a strange exercise, but hang in there. This will help you recognize the direction that your emotions are leading you in.

SITUATION	EMOTIONS

Now that you have identified three situations and the corresponding emotions they are releasing in your life, I want you to evaluate them in light of God's truth, *His Word*. Practice thinking through this process. Just because you experience an emotion does not mean the emotion is healthy and helpful. Measure it against God's Word. If the emotion leads you *away* from what God's Word says about your situation, then don't follow it. Learn to clearly identify what you feel versus what God says. Remember, what God says is always final, while emotions are often fickle.

EMOTIONS	GOD'S TRUTH/SCRIPTURE

PROSPERITY MEDITATION

Fortitude is the ability to take emotion and turn
it into energy for proactive, positive action.
It's not mere talk, but a fire that burns within
us to do what God has called us to do.

PROSPERITY DECLARATION

I am not ruled by emotions. Just because I feel something, this does not mean I will follow that feeling. Your Word, Lord, is my ultimate source of truth. No matter what situation I am facing and how I might be feeling about it, lead me to Your Word, Your truth, Your will. Help me to evaluate how I feel by what You say. I walk in courage and fortitude because I am led by Your Word and Your Spirit—not by my feelings.

Day Fourteen

HOPE

*Now may the God of hope fill you with all joy
and peace in believing, that you may abound
in hope by the power of the Holy Spirit.*
—Romans 15:13

PROSPERITY PRACTICE

When dealing with situations and circumstances, search God's Word for new options that birth hope in your soul.

We know that God is good, faithful, and loving. Perhaps we can even recite different Bible verses that back these facts up. However, when we start to experience opposition or difficulty, for some reason, it seems hard for us to hold on to these truths. This might be because we've never embraced the truths of God's Word as actual options for us. The Bible cannot simply be words on a page to you, nor can we view every single promise in light of "one day, someday in Heaven." God has given us His Word as a guidebook for living prosperously on earth (I hope by now you recognize the holistic definition of prosperity when I use the word).

Perhaps you have noticed a running theme throughout this session on Emotional Prosperity—the importance and vitality of God's Word in your life. Even though I provide some practical, specific keys for experiencing emotional prosperity, there is one key that stands out far above the rest—God's Word. Hope for a better tomorrow is cultivated by exposing yourself to God's alternative options *every single day*. Where are these alternative outcomes found for healing? Deliverance? Freedom? Stability? Joy? Peace? Salvation? *The Word of God.* Want to experience peace and joy? Follow Paul's advice. The God of hope will fill you with peace and joy *in believing.* All you need to do is take God at His Word and recognize that every truth and promise within Scripture is a new option for how you can experience a whole new way of living!

START PROSPERING NOW!

Think of *three situations* that you are currently struggling with in your life (maybe directly, or indirectly with another person/situation). Whether it is an addiction, sickness, form of mental torment or bondage, family or relationship issue, financial strain, etc., I want you to practice seeing each problem in the light of God's promises.

You are *not* ignoring the problem. But notice, I only provide a little space for you to list the problem and then three lines for you to write down the promise. Why? This is how we need to see our problems when measured next to the hope we find in God's promises.

Write down the problem. Then immediately, dive into God's Word and find promises that provide solutions to what you are dealing with. You can look in the concordance, use various online Bible resources, or even books that list out Bible promises by subject. Write down God's promises in relation to each challenge you face, meditate on them, memorize them, and keep them close by throughout the day.

PROBLEM	PROMISE

PROBLEM	PROMISE

HOPE DECLARATIONS FROM THE PSALMS

I want to provide just a few Bible-based hope declarations from the Psalms. I encourage you to do your own study, finding every passage that has to do with hope and identify what *new options* this hope release into your life.

My heart is glad and I rest in confident expectation that God's good purpose is being done in my life!

Therefore my heart is glad, and my glory rejoices; my flesh also will rest in hope (Psalm 16:9).

Lord, as I place my hope in You, You give me strength and courage!

Be of good courage, and He shall strengthen your heart, all you who hope in the Lord (Psalm 31:24).

I have hope that You hear my prayers and will respond according to Your Word.

For in You, O Lord, I hope; You will hear, O Lord my God (Psalm 38:15).

As I place my hope in You, Lord, my soul will become stirred to praise You! Hope awakens praise.

Why are you cast down, O my soul? And why are you disquieted within me? Hope in God, for I shall yet praise Him for the help of His countenance (Psalm 42:5).

My steadfast hope is in every promise and truth written in Your Word!

My soul faints for Your salvation, but I hope in Your word (Psalm 119:81).

I hope in Your Word—it reminds me that You, Father, are my hiding place and Protector. You are a shield around me!

You are my hiding place and my shield; I hope in Your word (Psalm 119:114).

PROSPERITY MEDITATION

Hope grounds us in the good things of God,
keeping our eyes looking upward to see what
God has for us on the horizon—instead of being
downcast, focused only on the problems of today,
or focused backward on the failures of yesterday.

PROSPERITY DECLARATION

My hope and confident expectation are in You, Lord. I trust in Your promises. I lift my eyes above my present circumstances and problems and focus on what You have said. I am more focused on Your promises than my situations. I do not pretend circumstances away; I just see them differently. I see them as a person filled with hope, which comes from knowing and meditating on Your promises!

Day Fifteen

TENACITY

*Keep on asking, and you will receive what you ask
for. Keep on seeking, and you will find. Keep on
knocking, and the door will be opened to you.*
—MATTHEW 7:7, NLT

PROSPERITY PRACTICE

Perseverance positions you to be relentless and tenacious in prayer.

Once we have hope, we will *ask* for the new options that Scripture reveals—and then *keep on asking.* Conversely, where there is no hope, there are no options to be tenacious about in prayer. Review the parable that Jesus shares in Luke 18:1-8 about the widow and the unjust judge. This woman was persistent because she had hope. She knew that the unjust judge was capable of giving her mercy from her adversary. Because she was exposed to this new option of receiving mercy from the judge (hope), she was able to be tenacious in prayer. She did not give up. She did not let her emotions get the best of her, causing her to spiral into depression or hopelessness. She fought. She persevered. She pressed in for a desired result. Fueled with expectation and confidence, she ultimately caused the unjust judge to deliver, not because of his good nature but simply because her "continual coming" wore him down (see Luke 18:5). Think about it. If the *unjust* judge delivered a good verdict on this widow's behalf, how much more will the Judge of all the earth who is holy, just, and perfect *"step in and work justice for his chosen people, who continue to cry out for help?"* (Luke 18:7 MSG).

START PROSPERING TODAY!

I want you to prayerfully think about any areas in your life where you have given up hope (or are about to give up hope). Use this page to freely journal about these things. Ask the Holy Spirit, the very resurrection power of God, to come and bring new life to hopes that have been deferred—or worse, destroyed. Pray:

Holy Spirit, come. Show me areas in my life where I have given up hope or I am low on hope. Remind me of Your promises. Come with Your mighty power and strengthen me to keep trusting You, to keep hoping. No matter what is going on around me, no matter what is coming against me, I pray that I would be a woman/man of relentless, tenacious hope. I persevere for Your promises to come to pass for Your glory! In Jesus Name, Amen.

PROSPERITY MEDITATION

The tenacious, even if they are not the most talented, intelligent, or gifted, stay the course and develop the skills they need to succeed.

PROSPERITY DECLARATION

I persevere for every promise that You have made available, Father. I am tenacious. I do not give up. Just like Jesus said, I ask and keep asking. I knock and keep on knocking. I am relentless. Your promises have filled me with confident expectation of a positive, joyful outcome. You keep me full of hope, and I will see Your promises come to pass.

Week 4

PHYSICAL PROSPERITY

Your soul impacts how you manage your body.

GROUP EXERCISES

SUMMARY

When it comes to discussing physical prosperity, this might be one of the most taboo subjects in the Church today. Many of us do what we can in an attempt to maintain our physical health. We aim to keep our bodies functional, but hardly anything beyond that. We attempt diets and fitness plans, only to give up and become disappointed. The problem is that we do not mark the direct correlation between our physical bodies and the prosperity of our souls. This session is all about giving you a clear vision for how the state of your soul directly impacts the condition of your body. The key to making lasting changes in your body is *not* trying to fix the problem at a "body level." The issue is much deeper. It is in the soul. When you have a healthy soul, your body will follow in its footsteps. In this session, I will give you some practical tips on how to experience physical prosperity, along with a resourceful acrostic that will help keep you mindful of these enriching principles.

LEARN

Watch Session 4: *Physical Prosperity.*

DISCUSS

1. How do you think the soul directly impacts the body?

2. Why do you think many Christians consider the body as almost a "taboo" subject?

3. In what ways does valuing your body as God's temple help you live a physically prosperous life?

4. Discuss reasons why you should value your body.

5. What traps can we fall into if we start believing that the physical body is not very important when measured next to the spiritual?

6. What does the following statement mean to you: Your body is the only vehicle that God has given you to live in—or inhabit—time. Discuss what it means to "live in time" and how your body is important to fulfilling this function.

7. Talk about some simple "action steps" to move forward with a plan for physical prosperity.

(At this point, ask some group members to share their testimonies of how they started down the road to physical prosperity. What were the first steps they took? How did they keep going? It is important to learn from those who have actually enjoyed a measure of success walking out the lifestyle that we desire.)

ENVISION

Describe what physical prosperity looks like to you.

Briefly write down a vision for what prosperity in the following areas would look like for you. Be sure to write down *only one thing*, as there are five categories. Don't let this exercise overwhelm you. Don't feel pressured to make overnight changes in every one of these areas. You can start with one. Remember, there is no pressure to perform. Describe your ideal vision for each of the following practices—how they might be integrated into your life and the benefit they would provide.

The Soul-Body Connection

Self-Control

Exercise and Nutrition

Rest

Purity

_____

_____

_____

_____

_____

_____

Day Sixteen

THE SOUL-BODY CONNECTION

Or didn't you realize that your body is a sacred place, the place of the Holy Spirit?
—1 CORINTHIANS 6:19, MSG

PROSPERITY PRACTICE

Begin to see your spirit, soul, and body as vitally interconnected. For too long, believers have emphasized taking care of the spirit at the expense of preserving the body. I cannot stress the importance of physical prosperity enough. Remember what you learned in our session together: your body is the special vehicle that God has given you to travel in time. The soul and spirit are eternal. They are without physical substance, and thus they are not time-locked. They will continue on forever, as they were created out of the eternal. Your natural body was not. Throughout the ages, this tendency has always existed in the Christian community. This comes when we believe the error that one dimension of our being is more important than the next, or that one is superior to the other. Your body is *not* evil. Physical bodies will actually be part of God's new creation, as we will receive resurrected bodies that will not die, tarnish, or wear down.

The substance of your flesh is precious to God, the very One who divinely sculpted you. One of the keys to preserving your body is maintaining your soul, and vice versa. The two are interconnected. What you do with and to your body matters, as it often gives the world a physical glimpse of the soul within. What's going on in your soul will ultimately be revealed in your body. This is why soul care is absolutely essential and our point of focus in your exercises today.

START PROSPERING TODAY!

Prayerfully consider any areas of your soul—mind, will, emotions—where you are experiencing stress, anxiety, confusion, fear, torment, etc.

Even though you might not be able to overcome them in a single instant, I want to help you recognize them. When you learn how to identify unhealthy areas of your soul, you can be on the lookout for things that might be harming you physically.

Simply write these areas down in the space below. Once you've identified them, you can be more mindful about intentionally allowing God to heal and cleanse your soul—and as He does, you will start walking in more abundant physical health as well.

PROSPERITY MEDITATION

While we can certainly implement different habits that
will contribute to our bodies being more prosperous
and healthy—how we eat, how we exercise, how
much we rest, etc.—none of that will do as much
good as implementing better habits of the soul.

PROSPERITY DECLARATION

*I walk in complete health—spirit, soul, and body. I do not
see one area as being disconnected from the other. Jesus, You
came to give me abundant life in every single dimension of my
person. Holy Spirit, help me to recognize anything in my soul
that is harming my body.*

Day Seventeen

SELF-CONTROL

A person without self-control is like a
city with broken-down walls.
—PROVERBS 25:28, NLT

PROSPERITY PRACTICE

Practicing self-control is not about the unhealthy things you are saying "No" to; it is about the prosperous soul you are saying "Yes" to!

The ability to exercise self-control is directly related to the condition of your will. The will is a powerful part of your soul, as it ultimately chooses what you do or do not do with/to your physical body. For the man or woman who is able to discipline the will, physical prosperity is truly waiting around the corner.

Often when we think of self-control, we view it through the lens of what we are not "supposed to do" or what we have to say "No" to. Change your thinking about this ASAP! The more you make self-control a form of legalism, the more you will resist it. No, self-control is never comfortable on the flesh, but there is a difference between being uncomfortable and utterly hating everything that you "have" to do. Instead, start defining self-control by the life-enhancing, prosperity-producing options that you are going to say "Yes" to. This gives clarity to your vision—and remember, the very foundation for this study is keeping a clear vision of what a prosperous soul looks like. When you see how saying "Yes" to nutritious eating and exercise actually protects your body—and therefore your soul—from deteriorating, you will be more inclined to enjoy making difficult decisions.

Remember, you are saying "No" to lesser things, only to say "Yes" to better things. You will more easily practice self-control by filling your mind with all of the possibilities that you are saying "Yes" to—I promise, it will make the journey much more enjoyable!

START PROSPERING TODAY!

List three areas in regard to your physical health where you see the need for more self-control. As you think about these areas and write them down, *do not feel bad, discouraged, or condemned!* This is a tool to help you work toward victory. The key is spending only a few seconds thinking of those areas, while spending *more time* reflecting upon your vision for what you'd like to see instead. If you struggle with exercise, get a vision of how you see your body benefitting from a consistent exercise routine. Likewise, if you have difficulty in maintaining a healthy diet, get a vision for how you could look, feel, and function by eating differently.

AREAS THAT NEED SELF-CONTROL	MY VISION

PROSPERITY MEDITATION

We must exercise self-control in choosing tomorrow's triumphs over today's struggles, pains, and instant gratifications. It is the basis for physical prosperity, as well as prosperity in every other realm.

PROSPERITY DECLARATION

Self-control brings me into new levels of abundance and victory. I feel great and look the way I want, not because it automatically happens, but because I practice self-control. I have a clear vision of what I am working toward and I will not deviate from it. I will not get distracted. I will not go off course. My eyes are on the prize—and by Your grace, I will experience prosperity in my health because I exercise self-control!

EXERCISE AND NUTRITION

I discipline my body like an athlete,
training it to do what it should.
—1 CORINTHIANS 9:27, NLT

PROSPERITY PRACTICE

By choosing a lifestyle of exercise and nutrition, you are making life-enhancing decisions that position you for health in every other realm of life and living.

God has a vision for your body. In fact, He has a holistic vision for every sphere of your life! He desires you to walk in prosperity of mind, body, and spirit. We have already talked about (in brief) what a prosperous spirit and mind look like. Now, it is very important that we emphasize the need to make daily decisions that position your physical body for prosperity. As pertaining to developing the body, Paul uses the word *discipline.*

Just as there are spiritual disciplines that build your spirit, such as Scripture study, prayer, and meditation, there are also physical disciplines. None of these come naturally, hence why they demand discipline (conscious acts of our will; making decisions that lead to a desired end result). A routine of exercise and a lifestyle of good nutrition will not come to you naturally. You won't wake up one day and *feel* like eating well and working out. You need to make vision-motivated choices to integrate these disciplines into your everyday life routine. I use the term "vision-motivated" because, again, you need to have a clear vision of the desired outcome that you want these disciplines to produce in your life. Without this personalized vision of your end result, you will not have the motivation to keep going on the days when you don't feel like it. Exercise and nutrition *demand* a resolve to train your body to do what it should. Your flesh must obey a determined soul. Just remember, your will has the ability to build new, life-enhancing habits in your life that bring you into new realms of prosperous living.

START PROSPERING TODAY!

Now, I want you to select *one goal* and *one actionable step* that you can take toward fulfilling your vision for a healthier lifestyle. Remember, it is important for you to start small and start *somewhere*. Don't overwhelm yourself with lots to do at first. The key to sustaining good habits is celebrating the small victories along the way.

My Vision for Exercise: One Action Step

_____

_____

_____

_____

_____

My Vision for Eating Healthy: One Action Step

_____

_____

_____

_____

_____

PROSPERITY MEDITATION

Change rarely happens until the pain of staying
the same is greater than the pain of changing.

PROSPERITY DECLARATION

*I have a clear vision for Your will for my physical health.
Father, I see myself the way You see me. You designed me to live
an abundant life. This includes being healthy, feeling good,
and having energy. You give me strength and self-control to do
what I cannot do in my own strength. Remind me of the vision
for how You want me to experience and enjoy life, Lord.*

Day Nineteen

REST

My soul finds rest in God alone; my salvation comes
from him. He alone is my rock and my salvation;
he is my fortress, I will never be shaken.
—PSALM 62:1-2, NIV

PROSPERITY PRACTICE

In the video session, I spoke about how you should live as if every day is your birthday. I know it may sound funny, but it is true. We need to live as though every day is a day of rest and celebration. This is the very *lifestyle* that Jesus brought all of us into.

The Sabbath Day, as pictured in the Old Testament, was a foretelling of the "rest of soul" that Jesus would ultimately provide for humankind. Throughout the Old Covenant, we see humankind constantly working to enter God's presence. Priests were always performing services. The people always waiting. Even though they had a Sabbath Day as part of their custom, there was a *Day* coming that would usher them into a completely new era of rest.

"Let us therefore be zealous and exert ourselves and strive diligently to enter that rest [of God, to know and experience it for ourselves]" (Hebrews 4:11 AMP). Does this Scripture confuse you a little at first glance? It talks about being zealous to the point of exerting yourself to *enter* rest. The work has already been done by Jesus. How do we enter this rest, then? Through steadfast, zealous believing. We need to stop trying to get rest, and learn how to take it. Rest is available *now*. I know people go away on

vacation or participate in an activity that puts them at rest. Afterward, they think to themselves: "I wish I could *always* do this." I have a secret for you. You can live *like you are on vacation* 24-7. If vacation puts your body and soul at rest and cancels out all the noise, hurry, and stress in your life, I want the soul-state that such a vacation produces to serve as an invitation for a new way of living.

The conditions of life will not always be restful—not by a long shot. However, you can make a conscious decision of will to orient your mind, will, and emotions toward the One who declared, "*It is finished.*" You can enjoy the most important, precious kind of rest imaginable—a rest that millions would empty their bank accounts to enjoy. Learn how to live mindful of the rest that Jesus has freely made available to you and use this as your invitation to enjoy *this same kind of rest* every day of your life, no matter what you are going through.

START PROSPERING TODAY!

Go through the Bible and find Scriptures about what Jesus has done for you. Write some of these key verses down and meditate on them. Remind yourself that Jesus performed the work of redemption. Your works could never save you, no matter how good. His work was complete and perfect and is accounted to you!

A good place to start would be Hebrews 4.

PROSPERITY MEDITATION

We do not get the rest we need if we are not living in God's cycles of grace, trust, obedience, and creative enjoyment in the tasks of each day.

PROSPERITY DECLARATION

I live every day in the supernatural rest of God. Holy Spirit, You empower me to imitate God, and God Himself is the Author of rest. He rested after the work of creation. Anytime I start to step out of rest, remind me of what Jesus did on the Cross. Help me to meditate on the work He did so that I can continually live at rest. May I experience the very rest of Heaven as I trust in His work and enjoy His refreshing presence.

Day Twenty

PURITY

*It is God's will that you should be sanctified:
that you should avoid sexual immorality; that
each of you should learn to control his own
body in a way that is holy and honorable.*
—1 THESSALONIANS 4:3-4, NIV

PROSPERITY PRACTICE

Pursue purity as a treasure that protects you from destruction and keeps you walking in God's promises.

Purity is *not* a limitation; it is your protection from compromise and destruction. Taking it a step further, purity positions you to continually enjoy God's promises. It keeps you along His path of abundance. Impurity does not remove you from God's love— surely not. But the choices that impurity produces can position you for destruction in your life. John reminds us that God's laws are not burdensome. (See 1 John 5:3.) In fact, God's laws are protective perimeters that help us live in the bounds of His abundance.

Let's examine a more contemporary rendition of the passage from Thessalonians: "*Keep yourselves from sexual promiscuity. Learn to appreciate and give dignity to your body, not abusing it, as is so common among those who know nothing of God*" (1 Thess. 4:3-5 MSG). Too often, we mistakenly see purity as a way that God holds us back from physical pleasure. Quite the opposite. Purity is God's way of helping you give dignity to your body. Those who know nothing of God tend to know nothing of their own worth before

Him. Whether someone is a Christian or not, he or she still has immeasurable value to God. God actually sent Jesus to die for this person. While God sees every human being on the planet as marvelously made and full of potential, we often do not share His perspective. As those who know Him, we must start agreeing with what He says about purity. One of the ways we do this is by actively pursuing it. Yes, *pursue* it. Many of us tolerate purity, thinking, "This is the way it's *got* to be until I get married." This is a misguided attitude. God's desire for purity is for your own well-being and happiness. By pursuing purity, you are not only making a statement that you agree with the precious thoughts that God has toward you—that you desire *only* His best in every area of your life—but you are also protecting your body from anything that would devalue or harm it or cause you emotional grief. Purity is Heaven's protection over the priceless treasure that is your body!

START PROSPERING TODAY!

I want you to start making a direct correlation between purity and God's promises. Think of some of the areas where God asks His people to walk in purity. Then, ask the Holy Spirit to give you clarity on what promise that decision of purity will produce in your life.

CALL TO PURITY	PROMISES OF PURITY

PROSPERITY MEDITATION

To walk in purity is to walk in singleness of
purpose, with your eyes open, pursuing God
and what He wants for you above all else.

PROSPERITY DECLARATION

*Purity positions me to walk in Your promises. It is Heaven's
key to experiencing the abundant, prosperous life that You
have made available to me. Above all, Lord, I choose purity
because I choose obedience. I choose obedience because I trust
You completely. You know the best path for my life. If you call
me into purity, then I know You are leading me along paths of
life, blessing, and protection.*

Week 5

RELATIONAL PROSPERITY

*You don't attract to yourself who you want…you attract
you who are. You resemble those with whom you assemble.*

Week Five

GROUP EXERCISES

SUMMARY

Everyone is talking about relationships these days! Why? More than increasing the quantity of relationships that we have in our lives, I believe we all desire to enjoy greater *quality connections*. Adding more people to your relationship circle is *not* the secret to walking in relational prosperity. In fact, adding more people could be destructive if you are assembling with people whom you ultimately *do not* want to resemble. Remember, you attract those who are like you. Do you want to enjoy deeper, richer, more intimate relationships? Are you tired of people who keep you in mediocrity instead of calling you up higher in life? The secret is *not* going out and getting new friends. The key to enjoying relational prosperity is simple: *Start with you.* When you change yourself, you will change the people you surround yourself with.

LEARN

Watch Session 5: *Relational Prosperity.*

DISCUSS

1. Why is it important to know that relational prosperity first begins with you?

2. What happens if you constantly change your friends/ circle of relationships but don't change yourself?

3. How are relationships a form of capital?

4. Read Proverbs 27:17. What does iron sharpening iron look like in relationships?

5. Describe how relationships have the ability to: 1) keep you where you are or 2) take you to the next level.

6. Can you share an example of a relationship in your life that: 1) kept you from moving forward or 2) positively pushed you into the next level?

7. How did Dr. Trimm's thoughts on rejection change the way you see it? Discuss how rejection can actually push you into new seasons and opportunities in life.

8. Reflect on times when you experienced rejection. Share about how that rejection turned around for your good and positioned you for a new level in life.

ENVISION

Describe what relational prosperity looks like to you.

Briefly write down a vision for what prosperity in the following areas would look like for you. Be sure to write down *only one thing*, as there are five categories. Don't let this exercise overwhelm you. Don't feel pressured to make overnight changes in every one of these areas. You can start with one. And remember, this should be an enjoyable journey. Describe your ideal vision for each of the following practices—how they might be integrated into your life and how they would prosper you relationally.

Empathy

Forgiveness

Kindness

Goodness

Agreement

EMPATHY

Yes, though I walk through the [deep, sunless]
valley of the shadow of death, I will fear or
dread no evil, for You are with me.
—Psalm 23:4, amp

PROSPERITY PRACTICE

Empower people by standing alongside them through their struggles and trials instead of merely feeling bad for them.

God demonstrates empathy *perfectly*. It is worth noting that there is a significant difference between empathy and sympathy. With sympathy, we feel bad for someone, but that is the extent of our personal investment toward that person. Empathy is something different altogether. While it genuinely feels, grieves, and weeps with another, it also reaches out with practical help. Empathy looks for ways to help people get *through* a struggle. David captures the essence of empathy in his timeless 23rd Psalm. He acknowledges that God, the Faithful Shepherd, is the One who actually walks with his people *through* the valley. Today, God uses you and me. We are filled with His Holy Spirit, and in turn we have the ability to be the hands and feet of Jesus to those who are going through some really dark valleys. To feel with them is one thing, but to walk with them is another. This is where we are invited to demonstrate the empathetic heart of our Father.

START PROSPERING TODAY!

Consider two recent relationship situations where you had to come alongside a friend or family member in the midst of a struggle (*where you were directly involved*). What was your response? Empathy or sympathy?

RELATIONSHIP SITUATION	MY RESPONSE

How could you come alongside this person and empower them *through* their struggle? (Start with small ways.)

RELATIONSHIP SITUATION	EMPATHY SOLUTION

RELATIONSHIP SITUATION	EMPATHY SOLUTION

PROSPERITY MEDITATION

It is much easier to do for others than to take the time to work with them, whether our children, our spouse, someone at work, or someone we are volunteering to help. We need to engage with others in such a way that is both loving and empowering if we are to interact with them as Jesus would Himself.

PROSPERITY DECLARATION

I walk in empathy in all of my relationships. When I see friends, family members, or co-workers going through difficult situations, I do not come in with idle words. I feel with them and for them, and I do whatever I can to help give them strength through their difficulty. Holy Spirit, thank You for Your wisdom that enlightens me. You show me how to model Christ in every situation so I can feel compassion for others, but also help bring them into a solution.

Day Twenty-Two

FORGIVENESS

*Let all bitterness and wrath and anger and clamor
and slander be put away from you, along with
all malice. Be kind to one another, tenderhearted,
forgiving one another, as God in Christ forgave you.*
—EPHESIANS 4:31-32, ESV

PROSPERITY PRACTICE

The secret to avoiding a bitter life and bitter relationships is choosing to forgive.

Remember, you will always resemble those with whom you assemble. To break it down even more, you will start to look and act like the people you hang out with the most. We often talk about how bad company corrupts good character (see 1 Cor. 15:33). I have to ask, then: Why do we even associate with bad company to begin with? Could it be that we are attracting those who act, think, and behave like we do? To enjoy relationships where bitterness is absent and forgiveness flows freely, you must set the example. This is what Paul was saying to the church in Ephesus. *"Don't wait for everyone else to put away wrath, anger, and bitterness. You take the lead. You set the example. Put it away from your life and replace it with forgiveness."* Bitterness is destructive. In fact, those who tend to carry bitterness attract bitter people into their lives. Everyone gets to be bitter *together.* The problem? Bitter is the enemy of better. If you want to move forward in life and become better, bitterness will hold you back. Follow

Paul's advice and put those things away. Bitterness is unhealthy and prevents you from enjoying relationships that will help you grow. I repeat, if you don't want to associate with bitter, unforgiving people, *take the lead, set the example, and replace bitterness with forgiveness.*

START PROSPERING TODAY!

We'll begin the process right now.

Identify where you are holding on to unforgiveness. You may have prayed about the situation or released this unforgiveness in the past—once or even multiple times—but I want to help you live in a place of constant freedom over unforgiveness.

Don't dwell on the hurt for too long. Simply think of the top *one or two* people/situations you still struggle with (that immediately come to mind), in terms of unforgiveness.

Write them down and pray:

> *I have released _____ to the Holy Judge. This situation is in His perfect hands. I have forgiven _____ (name the person or persons; remember to forgive yourself), because Jesus has forgiven me. As I have received Your forgiveness, Father, I pray that it would flow through me and empower me to walk in forgiveness every day of my life.*

#1

_____

_____

_____

_____

_____

_____

#2

<hr />

PROSPERITY MEDITATION

The road to freedom is paved by forgiveness.

PROSPERITY DECLARATION

Father, I decree that I walk in forgiveness just as I have received forgiveness. This helps me enjoy rich relationships. Father, bring me back to the Cross afresh and anew so that I can have a clear vision of what Jesus did for me. He paid the full penalty for every offense and every hurt ever committed. He took the retribution that I deserved. Thank You, Lord for making it possible for me to walk this same because of Your Son. As You have freely forgiven me of my sin, I choose to freely forgive those who have sinned against me.

KINDNESS

Three things in human life are important:
The first is to be kind; the second is to be
kind; and the third is to be kind.
—HENRY JAMES

PROSPERITY PRACTICE

Choose to display kindness at all times, especially when people don't deserve it.

Kindness is an opposite of bitterness. Bitterness is our poor attempt to poison another's life (which always fails, because bitterness rarely has impact on other people; its primary impact is upon our own souls). Kindness, on the other hand, is being intentional about giving someone something they may not deserve. Truth be told, none of us deserves kindness. God set the standard when He extended kindness toward the fallen human race—the very people who willfully chose rebellion in the Garden of Eden, and still yet, crucified His own spotless, beloved Son. After all of this, God continues to show extravagant kindness toward us through the ongoing ministry of the Holy Spirit. Consider Paul's words to Titus, where he describes the amazing kindness of our God:

> *But when the kindness and love of God our Savior appeared,*
> *he saved us, not because of righteous things we had done, but*
> *because of his mercy* (Titus 3:4-5 NIV).

117

The same Paul urges us to "*be imitators of God, as beloved children*" (Eph. 5:1 ESV). We have the ability to proactively demonstrate kindness to people—many of whom do not deserve it. According to Galatians 5, kindness is a fruit of the Holy Spirit. This means that the ability to show kindness is already present on the inside of you. You don't need to ask God for kindness. Even a prayer like, "Help me to be kind, Lord," needs to be reconsidered. We already have God's divine empowerment to be kind due to the Holy Spirit dwelling within us. Rather than spending time asking for kindness or even asking God to help us be kinder, *thank Him* for the supernatural ability simply to *be* kind. Step out, imitate your Father in Heaven, and start showing kindness toward those who don't deserve it. It is amazing how powerfully this displays the love of God to a watching world.

START PROSPERING TODAY!

Consider *three common scenarios* in your life where you are tempted to return *unkindness* for unkindness. We all have them. There are certain things that get on our nerves more than others, and when we get into these situations, we are more prone to become unkind.

I want you to list these types of situations and then come up with a plan for how you will supernaturally demonstrate God's kindness. Remember, *it is a decision*!

SITUATION	DECISION OF KINDNESS

PROSPERITY MEDITATION

We underestimate kindness if we see it
as anything other than one of the most
powerful tools of Kingdom expansion.

PROSPERITY DECLARATION

I will walk in kindness. Even though there are people and circumstances that frustrate me, instead of responding unkindly, I choose to draw from Your power, Holy Spirit. You enable to choose kindness, even when I don't feel like it. Father, reveal Yourself to the world as I demonstrate Your kindness. Show people that You really are good and that You do not respond to us the way we deserve.

GOODNESS

We should be astonished at the goodness of God,
stunned that He should bother to call us by name,
our mouths wide open at His love, bewildered that at
this very moment we are standing on holy ground.
—BRENNAN MANNING

PROSPERITY PRACTICE

Make a habit of focusing on and calling out the goodness inside of people.

Our culture is inundated with criticism, complaining, and faultfinding. It is so easy for us to spot the sin, the dirt, the shortcomings, the problems, the issues, and the failures. Truth be told, we all have faults. None of us are perfect! Scripture makes a very sobering case for this, just in case we need some extra reminding: *"There's nobody living right, not even one"* (Rom. 3:10 MSG). No one has it all together. We must recognize this as common to the human condition. This is the very reason Christ came to die for us on the Cross. Remember, we all start on the same level ground. None of us are good or righteous before God.

At the same time, God has created every human being in His image and likeness. Even though Romans 3:10 talks about our common sinful condition, the Creator wired us with amazing capacities, abilities, talents, qualities, and skills. There is beauty in every human being, because the Master Craftsman personally hand-crafted every individual. Goodness requires an effort from our end to look for the divine brushstrokes of the Master Painter in another person's life.

Here is the drawback of living in criticism instead of looking for goodness: The more you criticize people, the more you keep yourself trapped in bondage. You read that correctly. Criticism keeps *you* in a place of relational bondage. For one, it attracts the wrong kinds of "friends" into your life. They end up being people you can be critical with, spending the majority of your time engaged in gossip and talking behind other peoples' backs. This is *not* healthy companionship. Second, criticism prevents you from enjoying any true, deep, meaningful relationships. Even if you do have a clique of "friends" where all you do is gossip, chances are the same people you gossip *with* are gossiping *about you.* Look for the gold instead of the grime. We all have our drawbacks. It doesn't take special vision to see each other's mistakes; it does, however, take some intentional focus to see the goodness—and courage to call it out!

START PROSPERING TODAY!

List three people in your life whom you want to encourage. They may be really young in the Lord. They might be going through a difficult season. This does not matter. Speak to them. Write to them. Pray for them. Do all of these things, not to fix them, but instead to bring out the good already inside of them. Focus on the positives. Train your eyes to see the good. This will enable you to more effectively bring out the good *in them.*

INDIVIDUAL	ENCOURAGEMENT

INDIVIDUAL	ENCOURAGEMENT

PROSPERITY MEDITATION

We must let our cynicism be replaced with God's
goodness within us, and then cultivate it until
it can't help but pour out of us to others.

PROSPERITY DECLARATION

*I look for the good in every person and I call it out of them.
Protect me from cynicism, Lord. I will not define all people
based on my poor experiences with a select few. I look for the
gold and call it out. I see treasure in the rocky places. I summon
greatness in my brothers and sisters in Christ. I speak to their
potential, call out their goodness, and encourage them to step
into their purpose and destiny.*

Day Twenty-Five

AGREEMENT

*Can two walk together, except they be
agreed?* —Amos 3:3, kjv

PROSPERITY PRACTICE

Be intentional about cultivating unity through agreement.

Agreement in our relationships produces multiplied impact. Without agreement, we remain separate individuals, working by ourselves to accomplish separate goals. When we come together and collaborate, separate individuals join together to form a unit. This is the principle described in Deuteronomy 32:30, where we see *"one chase a thousand, and two put ten thousand to flight"* (kjv). The simple truth is that two people in agreement can get a whole lot more accomplished than two people on their own. The opposite is also true—for where there is strife, there is every evil thing. (See James 3:16.)

For there to be collaboration, there must be unity. Protect unity in your relationships at all costs. Nothing is more destructive to life-giving, life-producing collaborations than discord. Just as two individuals working in agreement can put "ten thousand to flight," where there is disunity and strife *nothing* gets accomplished. Whether it is two individuals, twelve people, or a company of hundreds, if there is strife, you are negating everyone's best efforts. Look for ways in your relationships to increase the level of agreement and unity. Whether it is in your friendships, peers, fellow students, ministry team members, or among your co-workers, be intentional to cultivate a greater culture of agreement. Not only is this the glue that holds groups together, but also a key that makes relationships—and organizations—more productive.

START PROSPERING TODAY!

Write down three significant relationships in your life. Now, I want you to vision cast. Imagine how greater intimacy, trust, and agreement could produce more significant transformation in both of your lives—and how your increased agreement could spread to your communities and spheres of influence.

RELATIONSHIP	WHAT INCREASED AGREEMENT COULD PRODUCE

PROSPERITY MEDITATION

Agreement doesn't happen until we can stand for
each other as much as we stand for ourselves.

PROSPERITY DECLARATION

I make every effort to increase the level of agreement in my close relationships—family, friends, church, my place of work, business (list specific relationships where you want to see a greater level of agreement). As I build greater trust and intimacy in these relationships, I thank You Lord that the possibilities become limitless. No opposition can stand against the great things You can accomplish through people living in agreement!

Week 6

SOCIAL PROSPERITY

*Social prosperity is not about the money you
make—it's about the difference you make.*

Week Six

GROUP EXERCISES

SUMMARY

When we have prosperous relationships, we will contribute to a prosperous society as a whole. This is what social prosperity is all about. As you learn how to walk in abundance, you will discover that you are a channel and catalyst through which prosperity flows. Your presence in society is a sign of that society's potential to improve. This is where many people confuse the prosperity message. When prosperity *ends* with us having good health, strong relationships, more money, a sharp mind, and other me-centered things, we have lost the very essence of what Jesus taught. We are not stagnant ponds that exist to accumulate; we are life-giving rivers that release the divine flow of Heaven into dry places. As we study social prosperity, I want you to think about it from this perspective. It is easy for us to complain about the many ills of society. They are surely obvious. Let's instead position ourselves to enter society and become agents of transformation.

LEARN

Watch Session 6: *Social Prosperity.*

DISCUSS

1. Discuss your understanding of integrity and credibility based on what Dr. Trimm shared in the video session.

2. How is reputation a key to your social influence?

3. How do credibility and integrity vitally shape your reputation?

4. Why is it important to have favor with both God and man?

5. Discuss the "keys to experiencing social prosperity" presented in today's lesson.

   • Why are people more inclined to follow you if you have vision?

   • As a leader, why it is important for you to know your purpose?

6. What are some ways that you can start adding value to society?

7. What does the following statement mean to you: "Social prosperity is not about the money you make; it's about the difference you make."

ENVISION

Describe what social prosperity looks like to you.

Briefly write down a vision for what prosperity in the following areas would look like for you. Be sure to write down *only one thing*, as there are five categories. Don't let this exercise overwhelm you. Don't feel pressured to make overnight changes in every one of these areas. Start with one. Take it slow and enjoy the process. Describe your ideal vision for each of the following practices—how each might be integrated into your life and the benefit they would provide to prospering you socially.

Integrity

Kingdom-mindedness

Leadership

Service

Justice

INTEGRITY

If it is not right do not do it; if it is not true
do not say it. —MARCUS AURELIUS

PROSPERITY PRACTICE

Behave the same whether people are looking or not.

In the video session, I talk about how integrity is expressed as you not lying to God *or yourself.* If you want to walk in integrity, it is vital that there is a oneness of thinking between you and God. Your thoughts should be in agreement with His. You should see yourself the way that He sees you. The essence of integrity is a consistent *sameness.* This is what the world is looking for. Likewise, you should walk before the world the same way you live behind closed doors.

As followers of Jesus Christ, we must demonstrate that this relationship is *for real.* It is not something that takes place on Sunday behind stained glass windows. Everything that Jesus has done *in* us must become manifest *through* us. There must be an outworking of our faith. Of course, we are not saved by any effort on our end. In fact, the very effort that it takes to believe the Gospel message actually comes from God Himself. We all stand before Him empty handed—but once we are saved, the story is different. It would be error to believe that we still stand empty-handed, as we have freely received grace, mercy, divine enablement, and the full resources of Heaven! For what purpose? To see the kingdoms of this world become the kingdoms of our God and His Christ! (See Revelation 11:15.)

This Kingdom transformation takes place as we *serve* society with our prosperity. The birthplace of this service is a people who agree with God's thoughts, embrace them as their own, and actually *live them out* every day. We cannot afford to "Amen" God's thoughts on Sunday and live opposite to them throughout the week. His thoughts are meant to influence every area of our lives so that we can in turn be prosperous assets to our world!

Start Prospering Now!

Spend a few moments in prayer and ask the Holy Spirit to reveal some areas of your thinking that need to be changed. Open yourself up to Him completely. This demands honesty and transparency. The Spirit of God does not come to condemn, but He does come to convict. The point of conviction is *not* to make you feel bad—it's to give you a glimpse of what normal looks like and empower you to experience God's normal in your every-day life!

Identify one or two problematic thought paradigms that need to be changed in your life. Then, delve into the Word of God and find specific Scriptures where God gives His thoughts/perspective on the matter. God's truth is what your mind *must* entertain if you desire to live with integrity. If you want to live like Him, you must first learn to think like Him.

MY THOUGHT PARADIGM	GOD'S THOUGHTS

MY THOUGHT PARADIGM	GOD'S THOUGHTS

PROSPERITY MEDITATION

To live in integrity is to pursue
living in God's best for me.

PROSPERITY DECLARATION

I walk in integrity and fulfill God's perfect will for my life. Any area of thinking that does not agree with God's Word, I ask You, Holy Spirit—reveal it to me and empower me to change my thoughts. I evaluate the thoughts that come into my mind. If they do not agree with Your Word and Your truth, I cast them down and reject them. Your thoughts help me to walk in Your will. As I walk in Your perfect will, I will make a difference in the world I live in!

Day Twenty-Seven

KINGDOM-MINDEDNESS

Behold, the kingdom of God is within you.
—JESUS, LUKE 17:21, KJV

PROSPERITY PRACTICE

Recognize that the Kingdom of God is within you—and make your everyday decisions based on this reality.

You are the most prosperous person in the world! Did you know that? If you have invited Christ into your heart, you have inherited an eternal, unshakeable Kingdom. The wealth and riches of this world don't compare to the splendor of God's Kingdom. If this is true, I am sure you are wondering: "Why do so many Christians live their lives as if they are the exact opposite of being prosperous?" Simple. We don't know what we already have.

Believers will become change-agents in every arena of society once they recognize that 1) they are citizens of a superior Kingdom and 2) this superior Kingdom is actually living inside of them in the person of the Holy Spirit. We recite the Lord's Prayer, *Thy Kingdom come,* with a faulty expectation of waiting for Heaven to do something for us. God is most certainly sovereign. Yet, in His sovereignty, He has invited you and me to participate in His transformational plan for the earth realm. When we pray *Thy Kingdom come,* of course we look to God as the One who releases the governing authority and power of this Kingdom. However, *where* are we expecting God to release this Kingdom? If we are looking up to Heaven, we are neglecting our stewardship of right now.

Remember that Jesus gave us a very clear definition of *where* the Kingdom presently resides—*within you*! There is a real, eternal place called Heaven. There is also a very real blueprint of order and operation that God Almighty desires to release into the earth so it functions as it was intended to—after the pattern of the heavenly Kingdom. God, the Holy Spirit, is the One who releases the Kingdom and *you* are the carrier of this Kingdom!

START PROSPERING NOW!

Make it practical. List some everyday ways that you can release the Kingdom of God in your life. (Some might be spectacular, but I want you to specifically focus on the seemingly ordinary ways—these are more powerful than you think!)

PROSPERITY MEDITATION

When you ask that God's will be done on earth
in the same way as it is in Heaven, you are asking
that things on earth be administrated in the
same way they are administrated in Heaven.

PROSPERITY DECLARATION

I am a carrier of God's Kingdom! My mission is to bring Heaven to earth everywhere that I go. This happens through both spectacular miracles and ordinary interactions. Holy Spirit, give me ears to hear Your voice and a heart that follows Your directions. May I live mindful that I am representing Your Kingdom to every person I meet and in every place I go. Help me to walk worthy of this assignment every day of my life.

Day Twenty-Eight

LEADERSHIP

Give away your life; you'll find life given back,
but not merely given back—given back with
bonus and blessing. Giving, not getting, is
the way. Generosity begets generosity.
—LUKE 6:38, MSG

PROSPERITY PRACTICE

Give away your influence and help empower other people to step into their destinies!

One of the best ways to maximize your leadership influence is to give it away to people who can never repay you. This is social prosperity at its best. You are making an effort to sow into the betterment of society by investing in someone else. By doing this, you are actually multiplying your influence! You may not think that you have any influence, or that your influence is insignificant. But just pause a moment and consider how what you have been given might help someone else. Always be on the lookout for these opportunities. It could be through writing a letter of recommendation for someone. It could be giving another person an opportunity to speak, communicate, or write for your organization. It could be given through an endorsement. It could be your mentorship, guidance, or advice. Think of what leadership influence you have been given and ask, "How can I give this away?" We cannot afford to keep our influence to ourselves. Your influence may be the very factor that empowers someone else to step into his or her unique destiny!

138

Start Prospering Now!

I want you to become generous with your influence! In order to reap increased influence, you need to constantly be sowing seeds. Use your influence in people's lives to encourage them. Empower them. Uplift them. Inspire them. Give them opportunity. Spheres of influence may include your job, church, family, or friends—any network of relationship that God has given you is your place of stewardship and your place of seed planting. Intentionally sow seeds of influence into your spheres of influence. Yes, you will position yourself for increase and promotion, but even greater will be the impact that your influence produces upon the lives you touch.

SPHERE OF INFLUENCE	SEED OF INFLUENCE

PROSPERITY MEDITATION

The best leaders rise not because of a hunger for
authority or a need to prove they are capable,
but by being effective influencers others
will look to for motivation, encouragement,
inspiration, and enablement.

PROSPERITY DECLARATION

I lead by sowing seeds of influence every day. Show me people and places where I can use my influence to make their lives better— their organizations flourish—their communities enriched. I bring Kingdom transformation by being a good steward of the influence You have entrusted to me. You are the God of promotion. You are the God of increase. Help me lead people to you and the fulfillment, transformation, and rich life You have waiting for to them.

Day Twenty-Nine

SERVICE

For even the Son of Man came not to
be served but to serve others.
—MATTHEW 20:28, NLT

PROSPERITY PRACTICE

Transform your world in practical and powerful ways by asking yourself, "How can I serve others today?"

We need to be known as the greatest servants to society! This is what it means to advance the Kingdom of God. In times past, when people have used words like "dominion" and "authority" in regard to bringing God's Kingdom to earth, there has been a gross misunderstanding that God's influence comes to society through takeover. This is not the case at all. Jesus was often found correcting His disciples for their faulty concepts of what it meant to advance the Kingdom of God in the earth. They struggled to see it from a spiritual perspective and, in turn, envisioned a violent overthrow of the oppressive governing structure of Rome. Even as Jesus was getting ready to ascend into Heaven, the disciples were asking Him questions like, "*Master, are you going to restore the kingdom to Israel now? Is this the time?*" (Acts 1:6 MSG). Even though it seemed like Jesus dodged their question,

He was, in fact, providing a better answer than their minds could fathom. Instead,

> He told them, *"You don't get to know the time. Timing is the Father's business. What you'll get is the Holy Spirit. And when the Holy Spirit comes on you, you will be able to be my witnesses in Jerusalem, all over Judea and Samaria, even to the ends of the world"* (Acts 1:7-8 MSG).

God gave us the Holy Spirit so we could continue the ministry of Jesus. What was His ministry motivated by? A desire to serve humanity, bringing the lost into relationship with His Father and empowering people to make society better by reflecting the culture and value system of Heaven more clearly.

START PROSPERING NOW!

Consider some ways that you can practically serve the people around you. Don't discount anything as insignificant because it does not appear grandiose or flashy. It does not matter, for all acts of service—motivated by a genuine compassion for helping others—carry the DNA of Father God and make an open display of His loving nature.

Write down a list of people, places, organizations, charities, etc. that you can envision yourself serving. You can't do everything, but you can certainly do something. It may not be complicated. In fact, I would encourage you to start simple! Brainstorm some ideas below and then pray about *one* opportunity where you can start serving. By serving another person, you are releasing the dominion of God's Kingdom into someone's life. There is truly no such thing as insignificant service!

PROSPERITY MEDITATION

Service is taking our place as God's
hands and feet on the earth.

PROSPERITY DECLARATION

I serve as an act of worship before You, Lord. I want the world to know You like I do. And if there are any areas in my life where I am not reflecting You accurately, help me to see You more clearly. Give me a fresh glimpse of Your goodness, Your compassion, Your love, and Your kindness so I can serve others more effectively.

Day Thirty

JUSTICE

*So let us come boldly to the throne of our gracious
God. There we will receive his mercy, and we will
find grace to help us when we need it most.*
—HEBREWS 4:16, NLT

PROSPERITY PRACTICE

You have been given a voice of authority before the Throne of
God to intercede on behalf of the injustices in this world!

It is truly overwhelming to be confronted with the many injustices
that are going on in the earth today. I hesitate to list them, as the
crimes committed against humanity are heinous. The poverty, war,
starvation, disease, and abuse that take place on a daily basis can
often produce hopelessness in our hearts. We cannot lose heart.
You may be asking, "*What can I do?*" Of course, I advocate for getting
involved, raising your voice, and playing a role in bringing justice
where there seems to be none. At the same time, there is a place we
can *all* get involved—the place of prayer. To some, this might sound
like a copout. Prayer only sounds like a copout when we fail to recognize the significant power that it carries and releases.

You have a voice before the very Throne of God. This is the position of an intercessor. Even though there are some in the Body of
Christ who feel a particular call to assume the role of interces-
sors, all believers can intercede on behalf of injustice. The blood
of Jesus has given you this place of access. But also know that your
place of access is also a place of authority. Many of us know that

prayer is a place of access before the Lord. He hears us and we hear Him. There is also a place of authority, where we discover God's heart, know God's Word, and start declaring God's decrees. This is not authority to tell God what to do. Not at all. Rather, it is a commanding authority to tell the injustices of this world what to do. When there is a standard in God's Word that people are living beneath or violating, we declare that the injustice will come in agreement with Scripture. We command injustice to bow before the perfect will of God.

There are unknowns and mysteries when it comes to the will of God, yes. However, there are also very clear *knowns*. By spending time in the Word, we begin to discover God's heart toward the different injustices in this world. This helps us to pray with confidence for injustice to come to a speedy end in Jesus' Name!

Start Prospering Now!

Even though we are bombarded with injustices on a daily basis, I want you to recognize your authority as a voice before Heaven's throne.

Take this time to write down some of the injustices that come to your mind and then pray. Pray God's remedy. Pray God's will. Pray for deliverance for those in captivity. Pray for healing for the diseased. Pray that the homeless and hungry would receive supernatural provision. And pray for ideas and strategies to help bring it all to pass. God will move in the earth—this is for sure. At the same time, He uses human vessels as catalysts to move through.

PROSPERITY MEDITATION

Justice isn't just a good idea; justice
emanates from the character of God.

PROSPERITY DECLARATION

You have given me a voice before Your throne of grace, Lord. I can come boldly and present before You the injustices that are upon my heart. You look down and Your heart is broken over these things, too. Thank You, Father, for using my prayers to bring hope and healing.

Week 7

VOCATIONAL PROSPERITY

God does not reward potential,
He rewards performance.

Week Seven

GROUP EXERCISES

SUMMARY

Your place of work is your place of worship. Your vocation is your ministry. It is time that we stop reducing ministry simply to those who preach from a pulpit on Sunday, but start seeing our everyday 9-to-5 as a place of ministry (instead of a place of endured *misery*). Too many of us are missing out on incredible opportunities to shine for Christ because we neglect the unique mission field that God has placed us in. You might be asking God, "Lord, I want to serve You better. I want to help people more effectively. Show me where I can do this!" Our ears listen for Heaven to give us some missions trip assignment or commission to volunteer at the local homeless shelter. We must, by all means, participate in these kinds of efforts. But what if God is calling you to go on a missions trip every single day as you walk into your workplace? This week, you are going to discover some practical tips to walking in vocational prosperity. Get ready to change your perspective on doing your job and learn how to experience abundance in your everyday, 9-to-5 career.

LEARN

Watch Session 7: *Vocational Prosperity.*

DISCUSS

1. Why do you think many Christians do not see their jobs or vocations as opportunities for ministry?

2. How can you start seeing your work as worship?

3. List some ways that you could "take the anointing to work." What could this look like?

4. Discuss the following statement: "Fire your job and go to work!"

5. What are some practical ways that you can change the way you think when it comes to your vocation?

6. How are you reading/studying about your discipline?

7. What is your present "Goliath" in the workplace?

   • Allow people to share about their struggles and obstacles at work.

   • Take time to pray together over these work-place giants. Pray specifically for perspective and empowerment. Too many people go after a quick fix, which is quitting their jobs. To quit requires tremendous discernment. The alternative to quitting is staying, facing your giants, and experiencing a new season of blessing where you currently are. Remember, blessing and promotion are often on the other side of defeating your Goliath.

ENVISION

Describe what vocational prosperity looks like to you.

Briefly write down a vision for what prosperity in the following areas would look like for you. Be sure to write down *only one thing*, as there are five categories. Don't let this exercise overwhelm you. Don't feel pressured to make overnight changes in every one of these areas. Simply start with one. Describe your ideal vision for each of the following practices—how they are integrated into your life and how each might prosper you in your vocation.

Purpose

_____

_____

_____

Diligence

_____

_____

_____

Investment

_____

_____

_____

Good Work

_____

_____

_____

Holy Ambition

_____

_____

_____

Day Thirty-One

PURPOSE

Lord, when I feel that what I'm doing is insignificant
and unimportant, help me to remember that everything
I do is significant and important in your eyes, because
you love me and you put me here, and no one else
can do what I am doing in exactly the way I do it.
—BRENNAN MANNING

PROSPERITY PRACTICE

Divine purpose is discovered, not when we receive full clarity on a specific assignment or calling, but when we recognize that work is worship and worship is work.

To sustain our vision and motivation at work—especially when we find ourselves doing the same thing, day after day—we must conclude that nothing we do is insignificant or unimportant to the Lord. Everything we do, from selling real estate, to curing cancer, to working a desk job, to accounting, to teaching kinder-garten—*everything* can be fueled by a sense of deep purpose and meaning. How does this happen? It all begins with perspective. I know many of us assume that in order to fulfill our purpose in life, we need to have clarity about some specific calling or work that we are supposed to do—our great assignment on planet earth. While God does have unique assignments for each of us (often times, there are *multiple* assignments), purpose begins when we understand that everything we do can serve as an act of worship. There is no higher purpose for all of our lives than

152

to give glory back to the One who made us, gave us breath, and placed within us the very grace to work. Purpose begins when we blur the lines that separate work from worship. Perform your work as a form of worship acknowledging the Creator who built within you the capacity to work. When you operate out of your created design, you are giving glory to God. Purpose starts with a worship perspective.

START PROSPERING NOW!

Consider your current place of work or area of vocation. Think of ways that God can fulfill His holy purposes through you where you are right now.

Write some of these possibilities down as the Holy Spirit leads.

_____

_____

_____

_____

_____

PROSPERITY MEDITATION

I embrace the fact that my "vocation" is a big part of my God-given purpose and deliberately release His spiritual wisdom, power, and creativity into everything I do.

PROSPERITY DECLARATION

I fulfill my holy calling wherever I am today. At my job. In my family. Whatever I have been given to do and to accomplish, this is my holy calling. Holy Spirit, help me to live in step with You. I hear Your voice, follow Your direction, and give You complete control over my life. Every day, you lead me into Your perfect will. May everything I do bring You great glory!

DILIGENCE

You can do anything...but not everything.
—DAVID ALLEN

PROSPERITY PRACTICE

Be diligent to focus on what is right in front of you—and do it well!

A key to diligence is focus. Although there is a time and place for multi-tasking, the secret is not allowing a number of tasks to prevent you from accomplishing what is most important. In being diligent, we need to have a plan for the future. We also need to learn how to delegate responsibility to others, when possible. But the most important thing you can do to practice diligence every day is forbid distraction in your work life. Diligence produces progress, while distraction constantly yields disappointment. People often live in a place of perpetual disappointment because they feel like they don't get anything done. Have you ever heard anyone say, "I was so busy today, but didn't get anything done!"? Maybe you've said this yourself! It is perplexing, because we all have been given the same amount of time in a day.

The problem is that distraction robs us of the joy of completing the tasks at hand. Diligence, on the other hand, protects us from ditches like distraction, procrastination, and even the so-called "tyranny of the urgent." Diligence knows what task is most important and accommodates it with excellence and undivided attention. The payoff is a job well done! This is truly an example of what it looks like to walk in vocational prosperity. It is not simply making money; it is about completing what is most important and having a deep satisfaction in your soul that you followed through on the assignment you were given—and did it well!

START PROSPERING NOW!

List some practical ways you can be diligent where you are today (at your workplace, in your business, etc.). Then, describe what you envision those acts of diligence producing. Remember, the results of your diligence will not always be immediate—diligence rarely pays off immediately. However, without diligence, there won't be any results at all.

ACTS OF DILIGENCE	RESULTS OF DILIGENCE

PROSPERITY MEDITATION

In whichever area of life you apply yourself you
will prosper—you will enjoy vigorous and healthy
growth in whatever realm of life you are diligent.

PROSPERITY DECLARATION

I am a diligent, hard worker. I do everything with excellence as I am working unto the Lord. Every act of diligence is positioning me for the next level—in my life, in my job, in my career, and in my calling. Help me to steward what I have been given to do right now, and do it joyfully, so I am ready for increase when the season of promotion comes.

Day Thirty-Three

INVESTMENT

While the earth remains, seedtime and harvest, cold and heat, summer and winter, and day and night shall not cease.
—Genesis 8:22

PROSPERITY PRACTICE

Your intentional investments of time, talent, and treasure have the potential to produce a harvest wherever they are planted.

In order to fully understand the principle of investment, we must go back to Genesis 8 where we read about the Law of Seedtime and Harvest. Later in the New Testament, Paul reinforces the continuing nature of this principle by reminding the Galatian church: "*Do not be deceived, God is not mocked; for whatever a man sows, this he will also reap*" (Gal. 6:7 NASB). When we don't invest, we don't have a vision for how the practice of investment produces a harvest. I am not simply referring to money here. I know Scriptures and principles like these have been often exclusively applied to financial increase in the past. Perhaps this is why so many of us don't see how applicable the practice of investment is in every area of our lives.

Specifically, you have the ability to invest your time, your talent, *and* your treasure. Because most of us have a basic concept of financial investment, I want to encourage you to be intentional about investing your time and talent. Have a vision for how the seeds of your investment could produce a harvest. Maybe the harvest will be in a co-worker's life. Perhaps the harvest will be in the company's overall advancement. The harvest could be that your division or your team makes significant progress on a project. Within the context of vocational prosperity, understand that your investment is powerful. It might just be a seed when you make the initial investment, but as you cultivate it, and as others help water it through their participation, it will grow into something brilliant!

START PROSPERING NOW!

Identify *one investment* you can make in each of the following three areas in regards to your vocation.

1. Time Investment:

_____

_____

_____

_____

2. Talent (Skills) Investment:

_____

_____

_____

_____

3. Treasure (Financial) Investment:

_____

_____

_____

PROSPERITY MEDITATION

Investment is a powerful Kingdom practice that multiplies your effect wherever you apply it.

PROSPERITY DECLARATION

I make wise investments in every area of my life. I recognize that the best investments produce a multiplied return. I do not waste my time, talent, or treasure with anything less than Your best. Help me to evaluate every decision that I make by whether it will waste, spend, or invest the assets and resources You have given me.

Day Thirty-Four

GOOD WORK

Nothing will work unless you do.
—Maya Angelou

PROSPERITY PRACTICE

Commit yourself to doing good work wherever you are, whatever you are doing—this will position you for increase and promotion in God's Kingdom economy.

On the first day of our week together, we were reminded that work is worship. It is the Lord Himself who gave us the ability to do good work. Laziness and idleness are frowned upon in the Scriptures, while there is a powerful promise reserved for the good worker: "*The Lord will send rain at the proper time from his rich treasury in the heavens and will bless all the work you do. You will lend to many nations, but you will never need to borrow from them*" (Deut. 28:12 NLT). Note that the Lord will bless all the work you *do*. We partner with God to create prosperity. The Kingdom does not operate as a get rich quick scheme—as most define "rich" anyway. There is no magic formula other than doing good work with diligence.

God gave us work not to burden, but to fulfill us. It is through work that we enjoy the richness of life and the many and various rewards of our labor. Not only does our work result in financial increase, but the actual work *process* is a source of prosperity. Your commitment to good work does not merely produce a paycheck; it develops your skills. You are built up as a person. You learn valuable principles about perseverance, dealing with failure, teambuilding, working with people, and drawing from the strengths of others. Eugene Peterson asserts that the "primary place of spiritual formation is the workplace." We are spiritually developed in the process of working and through the people we work with. Work is truly *good*. I know it may not feel like this all of the time. By no means am I suggesting that every day will be like a holiday. Even people who appear to have "dream jobs" have nightmare days. It is not about what you are doing, but rather *how* you are doing it.

God is watching how you steward where you are—right now. Are you going to commit to do good work, or will you grumble and resent your job or the people you work with? Or, will you continue to cheerfully do "just enough" with complacent mediocrity? The secret to supernatural promotion is not giving more money in the offering plate or praying really hard. Prayer and giving are wonderful, but if the person asking for increase or promotion is being a poor steward, he or she is not qualified for something bigger and better.

START PROSPERING NOW!

Think of three areas in your current job where you could adjust your attitude and position yourself for increased prosperity.

Adjustment #1

_____

_____

_____

_____

_____

_____

Adjustment #2

_____

_____

_____

_____

_____

Adjustment #3

_____

_____

_____

_____

_____

PROSPERITY MEDITATION

When we adjust our perspective and recognize that
we are working for God, not man, everything should
change about the quality of our labor. It should cease
being a drudgery and start becoming a delight.

PROSPERITY DECLARATION

*Whatever I do, I choose to have a prosperity perspective. I do good
work because I am working unto You, Lord. I enjoy my job, even
if it is not my dream career. I trust You, Lord, to promote me as
I purpose to be a good steward over what I have been given to do
now. I trust Your plan to fulfill my dreams when the time is right.
You are in control of my career; I am in control of my attitude
and perspective. Help me to trust You, work with excellence, and
enjoy where I am on the journey to where You are taking me!*

Day Thirty-Five

HOLY AMBITION

Whatever may be your task, work at it heartily (from the soul), as [something done] for the Lord and not for men.
—COLOSSIANS 3:23, AMP

PROSPERITY PRACTICE

Don't work for people; work for God and recognize that He wants to be present with you every day, all of the time—*especially* as you go about your work!

The above passage from Colossians perfectly concludes our week. We are finishing right where we started, reorienting our perspective about work. It will surely take some repeating to get this truth down into our souls: Work *is worship.* Work is not to be endured; it is to be enjoyed. How many people do you know who live out what Paul describes in Colossians 3:23? We are encouraged to work *heartily,* which literally means to work *from the soul.* Our minds, wills, and emotions are not sitting at a desk, wasting away while we function like drones from 9 to 5, Monday through Friday. Such is not a prosperous life; it is a stagnant existence at best. There is a difference between *living* and existing. Those who live are actually engaging their souls, while those who choose the path of existence simply go through the motions of life. They show up, speak when they are told to, perform to keep from losing their jobs, and eagerly wait for Friday every time Monday comes.

The secret to treating work as worship and working from your soul is maintaining a holy ambition. Paul captured his holy

163

ambition in the verse above—do your work as if you are working for the Lord and not for people. When you see yourself as working for God, everything changes. You learn how to become mindful of God every day, in everything you do—where previously, you may have only been mindful of Him during church activities and devotional times. The Holy Spirit is working with you. He will give you insight, clarity, and direction on the task that you are assigned to complete. He will give you supernatural wisdom to share with your supervisor or simply give you the ability to be there for your coworkers if they are going through difficult times. There are endless opportunities for God to receive glory through your vocation. Get ready to adjust the way you view work and experience the powerful presence of the Holy Spirit in a greater way... every day! Even though we tend to speak of ambition in a negative, selfish manner, when our driving life goal is to see Jesus receive glory in every part of our lives, such is a holy and commendable ambition that Heaven truly shines upon.

Start Prospering Now!

You can give God glory *right where you are* today!

Identify *three ways* that you can change the way you see your job and actually give God worship in the midst of what you do on an everyday basis. This all begins in your thinking. To live a worshipful lifestyle, you need to see your current place of vocation (even if it is not your ideal circumstance or situation) as an opportunity to worship God.

Three ways that I can worship God through my work are:

1.

2.

3.

PROSPERITY MEDITATION

One of the great lies keeping the Church impotent
and ineffective in the world today is that ambition
must be suppressed if we are to follow God

PROSPERITY DECLARATION

*I don't just go to work—I go to worship. God, Your glory is
my holy ambition. No matter where You have placed me right
now, I can experience great joy and satisfaction because I am
there to worship You. I am there to represent Jesus as Your
Kingdom ambassador in the workplace. May I worship You by
doing my job with excellence, modeling the love of Christ to the
people I work with, and being grateful for the job that I have.
Worshiping You is my holy ambition.*

Week 8

FINANCIAL PROSPERITY

The bottom line of prosperity is always souls.

Week Eight

GROUP EXERCISES

SUMMARY

Financial prosperity is the last realm of life on our journey to prospering the soul. While many people associate the word *prosperous* with money, meaningful financial gain is simply one expression of holistic biblical prosperity. When this is elevated to the top of the list, we quickly get out of balance. Likewise, when financial prosperity is altogether removed from the list, we are likewise out of balance. Remember, a prosperous soul impacts every single area of life, from our spiritual walk to our relationships, from our work to our overall impact in society, from our bodies to our wallets. The key is remembering the *purpose* of prosperity. God desires to bring increase into your life. He even delights as you enjoy the fruit of your prosperity. However, the overall vision for prosperity cannot be self-seeking. It cannot be living to accumulate, but instead living to give. When we assume the position of living our lives with hands wide open before the Lord, He will never cease to fill them to overflowing. He knows that open hands are giving hands and they are a safe place to entrust financial abundance.

LEARN

Watch Session 8: *Financial Prosperity.*

DISCUSS

1. What are some of the lies you have heard about money and wealth in the Church?

2. How can financial increase be a good thing when used for Kingdom purposes?

3. Describe how you can 1) experience financial prosperity, 2) enjoy the reward of your increase, and yet 3) live to be a giver? Is there a balance between these three?

4. Read Deuteronomy 8:18. How do you think God gives you the power to get wealth?

5. Which of the "keys to experiencing financial prosperity" stuck out to you the most?

6. How are inspired ideas a powerful starting place for financial prosperity?

7. How does solving problems produce greater prosperity?

8. What is the bottom line to financial prosperity? How do we make this "bottom line" practical in our everyday lives?

ENVISION

Describe what financial prosperity looks like to you.

Briefly write down a vision for what prosperity in the following areas would look like for you. Be sure to write down *only one thing*, as there are five categories. Don't let this exercise overwhelm you. Don't feel pressured to make overnight changes in every one of these areas. You can start with one. And remember, this should be an enjoyable journey. Describe your ideal vision for each of the following practices—how they might be integrated into your life and what value they would be in prospering you financially.

Being Content with Enough

Trusteeship

Storehouses

The Joseph Principle

The Life That Is Truly Life

Day Thirty-Six

ENOUGH

I know what it is to be in need, and I know what it
is to have plenty. I have learned the secret of being
content in any and every situation, whether well fed
or hungry, whether living in plenty or in want.
—PHILIPPIANS 4:12, NIV

PROSPERITY PRACTICE

Always be content with what you have, even while on the journey to financial increase and greater abundance!

One of the secrets to increase is contentment. When it comes to positioning yourself for more, I believe that God is looking for those who are using what they already have *well*, and also those who are enjoying what is presently in their possession. This is exactly what the apostle Paul was writing about in this verse. In every season, he was content. He always saw himself as having enough. Those who live with contentment look at their current level of abundance and celebrate it as being *enough*. Of course, we are all driven to pursue *more*. While there is certainly a healthy side to desiring greater increase in our lives, we can never let this impact our souls. Promotion is not a negative thing. Increase is not a bad pursuit. It is up to us to keep everything balanced at a soul level.

On our quest to acquiring more, we must live satisfied with what we currently have. Conversely, when our pursuit to acquire more is motivated by the deception that, "If I only had more, *then* I would be happy," there is a soul issue that needs to be addressed.

Contentment is a state of soul that sustains joy in every season, even while we are on a journey towards greater abundance. When the acquisition of *more money* becomes the only thing that motivates us, we have become a servant to something that should be serving us. Money by itself is not the root of all evil; the *love* of money is. When the quest for more money brings your soul into a state of bondage, you have forsaken contentment and are in dire need of a soul adjustment!

START PROSPERING NOW!

In the following simple exercise, I want you to write down everything you have that you are thankful for. When you are finished, review what you wrote and thank the Lord for blessing you so abundantly. Yes, He is the God of increase. Trust Him for greater opportunity, new blessings, favor, and promotion—absolutely. What keeps everything in balance is living a grateful, contented life. This is *truly* great gain.

PROSPERITY MEDITATION

There are only two relationships we can have with
money: Either we will serve it, or it will serve us.

PROSPERITY CONFESSION

I do not serve money, success, or material gain. I live every day thankful and grateful for the blessing You have made available to me. May I always focus on what I have, rather than what

I think I lack. I am blessed. I walk in Heaven's favor. I enjoy abundance right now. I believe You are the God of increase and promotion. I know You have wired me to succeed and enjoy good success! But Lord, I declare that my greatest success and source of joy is not pursuing things of this world, but in pursuing You.

TRUSTEESHIP

A person cannot receive even one thing
unless it is given him from heaven.
—JOHN 3:27, ESV

PROSPERITY PRACTICE

You become a trustworthy trustee in the Kingdom by being a good steward of what you already have; this is what positions you to receive divine increase!

God is watching how you steward money. Do you live with hands open and ready to give or fists tightly clenched around what you already have? I want us to further explore this concept of living "open-handed" before the Lord. Let's start by considering who God is and what He possesses. All of the wealth of the planet is His! In Haggai 2:8, the Lord declares, *"The silver is mine, and the gold is mine"* (KJV). The level of wealth at God's disposal is truly beyond your mind's comprehension! Taking it a step further, I believe the Lord actually desires to *entrust* His people with unusual levels of financial increase. The problem? For many people, this trusteeship would actually destroy them. God is all about contributing to *life*, not destruction. He wants to position you for success, growth, development, and maturity—not failure. For the believer who lives with hands clenched around what they believe is *theirs*, there is no real opportunity for divine trusteeship.

To clarify, I am not saying that God will send money out of the sky if you obey certain principles. However, God does reward obedience and stewardship by supernaturally using natural channels to release financial blessing. He can use your job as a vehicle for financial increase. He can release something into your life through an inheritance. He can bless wise investments. Yes, He can also unleash wealth into your life, supernaturally, as a result of your faithful giving into Kingdom ventures. He does not operate on a formula, though. He is not a vending machine, where you put in your money and then receive an abundant return by "pushing" the right button in prayer. You can pray, pray, pray, but if you are not a fit trustee for the wealth and increase of Heaven, God will not release increase. He is looking for those with hearts that are after *true* riches—souls being ushered into the Kingdom of God. When such is our motivation, our perspective is adjusted. Nothing belongs to us; it is on loan from Heaven. We get to enjoy it, yes. But in the end, it is all marked for a purpose.

God is looking for those who recognize this and live accordingly. Remember, increase is purposed to position you to be of greater effectiveness in the Kingdom. If God knows that increase will harm you, He will restrain His hand from releasing it. Likewise, if you live like everything in your possession is simply in your *trusteeship*, you are in a divine sweet spot where there are no limits to what Heaven can unleash into your life!

START PROSPERING NOW!

In what way can you live with your hands open before the Lord? Ask the Holy Spirit to help you identify any areas in your finances where there is a blockage or barrier to increase. Are you wrapping your hands around money that comes your way, holding on to it too tightly? Perhaps there is debt you need to pay off that is restricting you from maximizing your finances for other purposes.

Identify *two areas* where you can start working to "unclench" your finances and experience new levels of God's blessing and stewardship. Once you identify these two areas, put together a plan so you can begin enjoying freedom.

Area #1

_____

_____

_____

_____

_____

Area #2

_____

_____

_____

_____

_____

PROSPERITY MEDITATION

Every penny that comes into your possession is
for the purpose of expanding God's Kingdom.
Some is to give away to others working "full time"
in the ministry, and the rest is for you to use to
underwrite the ministry efforts of your own family.

PROSPERITY CONFESSION

*God, You own it all. May I live as a good steward of Your
finances and resources. Change the way I see money. All of it
is Yours and You have made me Your trustee—Your steward.
I live with hands wide open before You. This means I receive
freely and give freely.*

STOREHOUSES

The famine was over all the face of the earth, and Joseph
opened all the storehouses and sold to the Egyptians.
And the famine became severe in the land of Egypt.
—Genesis 41:56

PROSPERITY PRACTICE

Saving money is a way that you provide for and empower your future.

In this present generation, there is not much emphasis placed on the need for saving money. We all want to spend what we have so we can get what we want—*right now*. The problem is by immediately spending everything that we receive, we lose sight of the power that money can release into the future. Joseph supernaturally directed the Egyptians to store up resources because a season of famine was coming. Because of their commitment to save, Egypt became a source of life for neighboring nations during seven years of famine. One of the most powerful verses describing this scenario is Genesis 41:54, where we read, "*The famine was in all lands, but in all the land of Egypt there was bread.*" The entire earth was severely impacted by this famine; this was not some small, isolated issue. The impact of the famine was far-reaching. Yet, because Egypt did not waste the increase that was enjoyed during the seven years of plenty and instead made the decision to invest it in storehouses, the nation of Egypt became a blessing to *everyone*!

What is the practical application of this story? It is vital to get your finances in order so you can pay off your debt and start saving. You should be saving for difficult times, putting money aside in case of an emergency, job loss, or unexpected large expense. This is reactive saving, which we all need to do. I also want you to start proactive saving. Once you have an emergency fund set aside, you can begin *proactively* saving money, which is sowing seeds into your future. By doing this, you are providing streams of empowerment for years, decades, and even generations to come. You are able to empower your children to prosper by investing in their education. You can empower your family to live comfortably during retirement. By saving and storing today, you are digging wells that, when opened in their season, will become sources of life-giving nourishment for your dreams in the years to come, as well as divine resources to equip future generations for success. Never underestimate the empowering capacity of saving money. When those storehouses are unlocked in their time, they become springs of life!

Start Prospering Now!

List *one practical way* that can you start practicing the storehouse principle beginning today! Consider an area of your financial life that needs to be brought into order. Maybe you need to come up with a detailed budget that you diligently adhere to. Perhaps you need to begin paying off your debt (for an excellent resource on how to pay off debt, I encourage you to read Dave Ramsey's *Total Money Makeover*). Maybe the Lord is leading you to attend a financial class at your church.

In the space below, write down your *first step* to practicing the storehouse principle. Remember, it does not matter where you are; it's all about where you are going! Don't be discouraged if you are in a deep financial trench. If you remain diligent to continue these practices, you will quickly go from a state of lack to a state of increase.

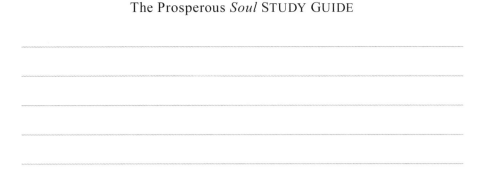

PROSPERITY MEDITATION

God blesses us and everything we set our hands to when we follow His mandates for how to manage His money.

PROSPERITY CONFESSION

I practice the storehouse principle. Wherever I am right now financially, I thank You, Father, that You can position me for increase, blessing, and prosperity. I declare that I make godly financial decisions that sustain me through difficult times and also lead me and my family and my business into greater levels of Your blessing. I am not discouraged. Wherever I start in the journey, You are with me. You give me grace, strength, and wisdom to experience Your best.

Day Thirty-Nine

THE JOSEPH PRINCIPLE

Then Pharaoh said to Joseph, "Inasmuch
as God has shown you all this, there is no
one as discerning and wise as you."
—Genesis 41:39

PROSPERITY PRACTICE

Saving is not just a financial action; it is a condition of the soul that operates by wisdom and discernment.

Saving is not just an action we take concerning how we handle money; it is motivated by the condition of our soul. How many of us have attempted to save money for a time, but only found ourselves stuck back in old cycles of acquiring money and then instantly spending it? This is typical, so please, do not receive this as condemning or accusatory. The goal is to empower you, at a soul level, to embrace the soul-ular infrastructure that was present in Joseph. At a soul level, Joseph was a man of excellence. The reason he was able to make good investment decisions with the increase Egypt received during the season of abundance was simple: He was discerning and wise. (See Genesis 41:39.) Joseph's internal characteristics transformed his external circumstances. It was Joseph's character that lead Egypt to become a source of life during the seven years of famine. In the same way, God wants *you* to be a source of life—to yourself, your family, your friends, your church, your city, and your world. Consider Joseph's perspective. During the years of plenty, he did not spend recklessly; he saved. Egypt used the resources that it needed in order to continue as normal, but saved up one-fifth of all the land's produce during the years of plenty. (See Genesis 41:1-36.) As a result, there was provision during the years of famine—a famine that had the potential to completely destroy Egypt and the surrounding lands.

In order to live by the *Joseph Principle* in our own lives, we need to take a brief soul inventory, get to the root issues, and honestly ask ourselves: "Why do I keep spending money instead of saving it? Is there a lie that I am believing? Am I compelled to live like everyone else because of envy or jealousy? To have what they have? Live how they live? Drive what they drive?" Oftentimes, the reason we don't save has to do with the pursuit of immediate gratification. We want to immediately have what everyone else has so we "measure up." This is where we get the phrase, "Keeping up with the Joneses." Let's cast off this way of thinking. By saving, you are choosing to live an extraordinary life today that positions you for exponential prosperity in the future! Like Dave Ramsey often says, "If you will live like no one else, later you can live like no one else." By embracing *The Joseph Principle,* you are saying: "Yes, I want to live like no one else!" We see what happened in the case of Joseph and Egypt. He made an extraordinary decision to save resources that positioned Egypt to be a source of refuge, help, and prosperity for others, even in the midst of an overwhelming, worldwide famine!

START PROSPERING NOW!

Write down and describe your vision of the extraordinary life that is possible for someone who lives by the *Joseph Principle.*

PROSPERITY MEDITATION

The person who saves when others are
spending will then have a surplus to buy at a
bargain when others are desperate to sell.

PROSPERITY CONFESSION

*I have an extraordinary spirit, and this positions me for
extraordinary opportunity. Just like Joseph, I choose to be
excellent—no matter where I am or what I am doing. I
operate in the wisdom of God. I don't go with the flow. I don't
manage money like everyone else. Lord, I choose to live by Your
principles of prosperity. As a result, I walk in Your abundant
blessing and am a source of blessing to others.*

Day Forty

THE LIFE THAT IS TRULY LIFE

*I came that they may have and enjoy life, and have
it in abundance (to the full, till it overflows).*
—JESUS, JOHN 10:10 AMP

PROSPERITY PRACTICE

Make sure that your vision for abundant, eternal life is in agreement with God's—and start enjoying it today!

We have come to our last day together! Even though we are still talking about financial prosperity, I want to wrap up our study with a definition of *true life*. The principles are certainly applicable to material wealth, as Jesus came to release His resurrection life into every area of our being—including our finances!

First, consider what Jesus *did not do*. Jesus did not come to earth, die on the Cross, and rise from the dead so you could lag through life. Seriously consider it. God Almighty did not pay the highest price conceivable—exchanging His precious Son for the redemption of humanity—so you and I could sleepwalk through our existence on earth. I agree, the Cross is *not* some divine ticket into a happy-go-lucky life where we get everything we want and God becomes our cosmic bellhop. This is a gross, perverted view of prosperity. The Cross eternally destroyed the barrier between you and God so that you could enjoy right standing with Him, and get this—start enjoying eternal life *today*.

Reflect on Jesus' unique definition of eternal life: "*This is eternal life, that they may know You, the only true God, and Jesus Christ whom You have sent*" (John 17:3 NASB). Eternity does not begin in Heaven; it starts the moment you give your life to Christ! Sadly, too many believers have been waiting for Heaven in order to start experiencing eternal life. This does not need to be the case!

Because Jesus rose from the dead, you can also live out a resurrected life. Paul reminds us that the same power that raised Jesus from the dead lives in us! (See Romans 8:11.) The prosperous soul is simply a life that is constantly under the influence of Jesus' resurrection. Every area that we have studied in our time together is touched by His resurrection power. Where there was previously death, lack, and defeat, there is now life, abundance, and victory. This is your inheritance as a believer. We only live below this standard when we have a weak definition of *abundant life*.

Abundance is not about waiting for Heaven to experience eternal life; it is enjoying eternal life today!

Abundance is not about getting more money or things; it is about Heaven's provision gracing every area of your life right now.

Abundance is not *all about me*; it is the way that I become a greater channel of God's love, goodness, and service to a world in need.

In short, this complete study was designed to give you a clear vision of what the abundant, prosperous life looks like! Remember the words of Proverbs 29:18: "*Where there is no vision, the people perish*" (KJV).

You may have concluded this study, but you are only beginning a journey that will lead to greater wholeness, blessing, wealth, and richness in every single area of your life. The question: "*Do you have a vision for it?*" Do you have a vision for richness in your spiritual life? In your relationships? In your finances? In your workplace?

There is a measure of divine living that God is inviting you into that is beyond anything you could ever hope, dream, or imagine. Get ready to start experiencing the life that is *truly life* and enjoy Heaven's abundant richness!

START PROSPERING NOW!

Review your vision of prosperity for each of the eight realms of life and clearly state them below.

Spiritual

_____

_____

_____

_____

_____

_____

Intellectual

_____

_____

_____

_____

_____

_____

Emotional

_____

_____

_____

_____

_____

_____

Physical

Relational

Social

Vocational

Financial

PROSPERITY MEDITATION

"What counts in life is not the mere fact that we have lived. It is what difference we have made to the lives of others that will determine the significance of the life we lead." —Nelson Mandela

PROSPERITY CONFESSION

I have a clear vision of what prosperity looks like in every area of my life. This is my goal—to live a life of worth—the life that is truly life! I will take this journey one day and one practice at a time. I will not get overwhelmed. I won't try to change everything in a single day. It is a journey. Thank You, Lord, for walking with me into this journey of prosperity. Give me strength when I am weary and feel like I can't go on. Give me wisdom to make life-enhancing decisions. And grant me the grace to experience the rich life that You have made available!